Creative Teaching

Also available from Continuum

Letting the Buggers be Creative – Sue Cowley
100 Ideas for Teaching Creativity – Stephen Bowkett
Creative Teacher's Toolkit – Brin Best and Will Thomas
Creativity and Education – Anna Craft, Bob Jeffries and
    Mike Leibling

Creative Teaching
Getting it Right

David Starbuck

continuum

Continuum International Publishing Group

The Tower Building
11 York Road
London SE1 7NX

80 Maiden Lane
Suite 704
New York, NY 10038

www.continuumbooks.com

British Library Cataloguing-in-Publication Data
A catalogue record for this book is available from the British Library.

ISBN 0–8264–9158–8 (paperback)

Library of Congress Cataloging-in-Publication Data
A catalog record for this book is available from the Library of Congress.

Typeset by Fakenham Photosetting Limited
Printed and bound in Great Britain by MPG Books Ltd, Bodmin, Cornwall

Contents

Contents

1 Being creative

Introduction: What is creative teaching?

'Pardon?' said the schoolteacher, his eyebrows arching like little horseshoes. 'You want me to like the buggers?'

'No,' said the slightly embattled education consultant, 'I merely suggest that you might like to give your pupils something other than lots of writing to do.'

'What?' the schoolteacher's rather large, heavy-looking moustache looked as if it was about to take off. 'What would be the point of that?!'

'Well, they might learn better and enjoy your subject more.' The education consultant, in her naturally optimistic manner smiled a tired smile.

'Good gracious, what would be the point of that?!' grunted the schoolteacher. As he marched down the corridor he chuckled and mused to himself, 'Imagine if pupils actually wanted to learn, how preposterous.' He entered his classroom, slammed the door behind him, and began ranting at his pupils about how lazy they were and how they did not take his subject seriously enough.

Creative teaching is when you appeal to the creative side of pupils' brains. If you would like to read some of the science, I've explained it in fact box 1 (pp. 4–6). Creative teaching can take many forms. Pupils may be in or out of their seats, they may be talking or working in silence, they may be working with you, in teams or by themselves. Creative teaching does not necessarily mean that you need to put in hours of preparation for every single activity you do, making up cards, activity packs and the like. This would in fact be a bad plan, as the pressure would remove any possibility of having a life outside of the classroom. While pupils might find it hard to believe that such a life exists, we teachers know that it does exist and that it is very precious to us!

The idea behind creative teaching is to enhance the learning process, and as such it should enhance your job too. It should be a satisfying and enjoyable experience for you as well as your pupils. It's not selfish to want to enjoy your job.

Creative teaching is a mindset to enter into: consciously entering into what I call a *creative state*. It's about how you present yourself as someone who cares and enjoys teaching your subject; how you motivate your pupils to participate and understand; how you go about making learning more fun or engaging. It's about spotting opportunities to liven things up. It's about encouraging pupils to take responsibility for their work in a way that doesn't feel like a burden (to you or the pupil!).

It is very easy for a teacher to get into a more protective, controlling mindset whereby every pupil's precise movement is contrived and dictated. Pupils have to do exactly as the teacher says, do the prescribed activities that are designed to keep them in their seats and not talk to anyone, and lack right-brain creative input. Often it's something we start when the pupils are young, and then never changes as they grow up. Or it's because class behaviour isn't very good and we feel this is the only way to achieve any form of coherent structure for learning.

Creative teaching, done right, will move you beyond such comfort zones into areas of teaching that are far more rewarding for you and your pupils alike. It requires a certain amount of trust between you and them. This is not possible, of course, without a clear and well-enforced discipline structure in place first, otherwise there's chaos. Getting the conditions right first is the most important factor when teaching creatively.

Creative Teaching

Fact box 1: Why teach creatively?

Actively noticing

Imagine that you've just bought a new car. You think it's an unusual car to have because you haven't seen too many of them about town. So why is it that when you drive your car out of the dealers, you notice at least half a dozen cars identical to your own?

Well, it's because your mind is 'actively noticing'. It sounds like a silly thing to say, but that is what it is doing. Pretty much at the hub of all your brain's activity is the *reticular activating system*, or RAS for short. It is the filter for all of your internal thoughts and for all the external information that comes through your senses. It's the bit of your brain that decides what you will and won't be conscious of. It tends to give priority to things that are new or surprising, and enables your mind to focus on things you find relevant or interesting. Hence the reason for being unable to stop yourself drifting off during a particularly long and boring lecture. Or finding it hard to concentrate when hungry or thirsty.

Logic and creativity

One way to ensure that a pupil's RAS doesn't filter you and your lessons out is to tap in to the different areas of their brains. We know that different sections of the brain are responsible for different tasks, and we know, broadly speaking, that the brain operates in two main ways: creatively and logically.

Although it is often said that your brain has two *halves* – a creative right half and a logical left half – this is purely figurative language. In reality, the creative and logical functions of your brain intermingle all over the place. But as it is quite convenient to talk about right-brain (i.e. creative) and left-brain (logical) functions then I shall use those terms.

Right-brain, creative, activities involve anything that taps into imagination, imagery, rhythm and rhyme. Whether you are running a guided imagery exercise, or getting the class to rap, draw sketches, or simply watch a good video, you are tapping into their right brains. Conversely anything that is text-based, or involves ordering and sequencing is left-brain. Solving simple maths puzzles, making a flow diagram and simply reading from the textbook are left-brain activities.

However, creativity is no good without order, and logic is not productive without an imaginative spark; so the two 'halves' need to form neural connections between each other to operate effectively and understand things fully. Tasks that use both sides of the brain stimulate neural connections and therefore tend to grab students' attention. Memory tends also to work best when the mind is engaged with the topic and the tasks. There are many ways to tap into the left–right mix, such as more complex/creative maths puzzles, teamwork, making association maps, or other diagrams that have an artistic element, drama sketches, role-play and creative writing. Later in this book we will look at preferred learning styles and multiple intelligences which also tap into the left–right brain mix.

Creative Teaching

Improving learning performance

Plenty of research tells us that a more creative approach to learning improves results. If pupils have an awareness of how they learn and an interest in the learning process, they take more care and control of their work. It gives them a sense of ownership over their work; it becomes personal. And we all know that as soon as you care about something personally, you focus better on it and perform better as a result. In terms of pupil learning, we'll call it improving their *learning performance*: their focus, energy, enthusiasm, comprehension and academic results.

The Campaign for Learning has spent several years researching 'Learning to Learn' in around 30 schools and has now started to publish its findings. Visit its website, www.campaign-for-learning.org.uk, to find out more. Essentially pupils and staff in these schools were given a lot of training about how pupils learn and how they can manage their learning. These Learning to Learn pupils have shown some remarkable development compared to other pupils not trained in these techniques. Teachers report that their pupils are:

- much more adept at processing knowledge, taking the initiative and self-evaluating their learning performance

- more motivated, reflective and resourceful
- enjoying learning more than they did and their self-confidence has grown
- communicating and working with others better than before
- remembering and understanding what they are learning better than before

These are not anecdotal findings; these have been backed up by tests and comparisons that show an improvement in school results as well as ethos.

In order to have Learning to Learn pupils you also need Learning to Learn teachers working in a Learning to Learn school. Teachers need to involve and appear to value all their pupils, be a good role model and create a positive, motivating learning environment. Such an environment is *best* enabled by a school-wide approach to Learning to Learn, so that the same attitudes permeate the whole-school ethos and are not restricted to individual classrooms.

My company, Learning Performance, has been visiting schools since 1994 to train pupils and staff in Learning to Learn techniques. In that time we have visited around half of all the UK's secondary schools; many of them value our regular input as part of their efforts to make pupils aware of the learning process and empower them to take interest in and control over their learning. It's from our experience presenting our workshops that this book has materialized. You see, a visit to a school gives a valuable snapshot of life in that school. What does it do to promote good learning habits? How happy and motivated are the teaching staff? How on-the-ball are the pupils? How much value is placed on keeping the building looking nice and creating displays that assist learning? How low or high are expectations of pupils and, for that matter, teachers?

This book is designed to provide practical ideas for getting creative learning and teaching techniques right in both the classroom environment and in the whole-school environment. This book should provide you with a useful bank of ideas that could be implemented in your classroom and in your wider school to promote a more creative approach to learning. Please do not expect a range of 'off-the-shelf' activities for you simply to emulate in your lessons. There are activities to get you started, but the point of this book is to help you get into a frame of mind that enables you to be more creative under your own steam.

Maybe you are reading this book solely for your own benefit, or maybe you have got together with a team of like-minded teachers to implement strategies and ideas; this book should be helpful in both cases.

Feeling creative

You are creative. No excuses, it's official. Creativity is something we all have; we now know that it is a skill that can be learned. It is not simply a gift given to the Mozarts and Einsteins of the world. You might not be as in touch with it as you once were as a child. You might never have had nurtured in you the creative touch that others seem to have. Or maybe you know there's a creative genius in you that is itching to be let free in the classroom. But take a moment to consider just how creative you and all those people around you actually are.

Think about it – surely a single parent is creative? Managing to cope when one person is doing what two people would normally do. What about your pupils when they go skateboarding or when they're getting excited about things that have happened to them? Surely they've connected with their right brains? What about when you need to work out the solution to a problem? Do you just sit and stress or do you think around the problem to find your solution? What about when you teach? It takes a certain amount of creativity to stand up in front of a class, hold pupils' attention and deliver a lesson. No matter how much more creativity you want to inject into your lessons, you should give yourself some credit here and appreciate what a good job you already do. How many people have told you that they couldn't do what you do? They have the greatest respect for your profession/relentless optimism/bravery and it is down to a certain amount of creativity and perseverance that you have already realized and they have yet to.

Tapping into natural creativity and harnessing it is an excellent way to solve the problems of our twenty-first-century lives. Now more so than ever because our world today is full of uncertainties – just think of terrorism, increasing awareness about child behavioural issues and the possibilities of technology – all of it makes life in the Western world at once more exciting and scary.

This is a fundamental reason behind the modern ethic that suggests that pupils today must learn how to learn. If they do so, the theory suggests that pupils in their adult lives will be better placed to handle the twenty-first century's advances and regressions with a creative independence. It is clear that people today no longer learn a trade at school or university and gain a job for life in that field. Everything is constantly evolving, and individuals need to evolve at the same time in order to keep up. Creativity is the key to successful independent learning, and it is through creative teaching that pupils will best get a feel for creative learning. Creative teaching can have many benefits, but it's not just a case of making pupils' learning experience more fun, about 'edutainment'. You can do a great deal to make your pupils' future much brighter by empowering them to know how they learn, and how to learn independently.

Of course, it is not always easy to feel like being creative in the classroom. You might feel tired instead; you've just gone through a pile of marking, your Year 11 reports are due, and you've got lunch duty to do which eats into your lunch break (which you were going to spend marking and writing reports). It's all very well reading this book, and have me tell you all about how to get creative teaching right, but what's the reality of actually finding the energy to do any of this?

Well, before you put the book down and give up, read this next section. It's about how to 'feel' creative. It is necessary to get the conditions right to teach creatively and there are several factors to consider: your pupils, your classroom, even your school, but most importantly there's you. I said earlier that creative teaching does not have to involve spending lots of time preparing things like playing cards or PowerPoint presentations; it is more about how you approach teaching a topic. There's a frame of mind that you can enter into which will, regardless of how tired or stressed you are, overcome any such distractions and enable you to do some fabulous teaching, often quite spontaneously.

I call it your *creative state*.

You can call it what you like, it can't hear you. If you want to call it something more floaty and, well, creative, then you could refer to it as bathing in your *radiant inner glow*. If you want something more down-to-earth, then how about *being-creative-as-opposed-to-being-annoyed-with-your-pupils*? Suffice it to say, I'm going to stick with *creative state*. It's simply a mindset to enter consciously into whenever you walk into a classroom, or approach a scheme of work, a new lesson or even marking.

Let's spend a little time forming this creative state in you. We need to consider a couple of things. First, we need to consider your stress levels and some relaxation techniques. Second, we need to consider how much you know about how people learn, and how this affects your pupils and your teaching. The idea is that whenever you approach your classroom, you will be more conscious of this bank of knowledge and its application and you will combine it with a more relaxed, alert presence of mind. Thus you have the building blocks of a more successful creative approach.

Later in this book we'll consider more things you may need to be aware of professionally in terms of how you relate to and motivate pupils, the types of activities you set and how you structure your lessons. But before we get into the realms of the practical, let's consider your mindset, your creative state.

The causes of stress

Take any school, from the top private school through to the toughest inner-city school, and there is one thing teachers will have in common: they're stressed to one degree or another. It can be for a whole variety of reasons and at a whole range of levels. In private schools teachers are under enormous pressure to 'magic' top grades out of all their pupils somehow, and any failure to do so is a poor reflection on themselves as professionals. In the toughest inner-city schools, stress often comes from dealing with seriously bad behaviour, whether it is aggression directed towards you, your colleagues or between pupils. In any case there's the report writing and endless marking, the clubs and other extracurricular things you do, dealing with exam boards, stacks of paperwork that never seems to be that constructive, being aware of individual pupils' special needs, chasing homework and coursework, dealing with parents, dealing with senior management (!) and just basically managing to teach something despite everything else that regularly gets in the way.

Do not think otherwise: teaching is one of the most stressful professions in the world. All that energy from hundreds of pupils: channelled well or badly, it is still energy and young people have it in far more abundance than any adult and, whether it is fun, charming, annoying or terrifying, it can really wear you out. Plus there is all the frustration from dealing with young individuals whose priorities are not your own and are often quite inconsistent. Most teachers have more right-brain creative leanings than left-brain systematic leanings (why else would you rather work with children than in an office?), so things like staffroom politics and dealing with the administrative side of teaching tend to be a source of aggravation and avoidance rather than something that is par for the course.

So how does stress work? How can it be a good thing and how does it become a bad thing? How do you manage stress as a professional?

Let me tell you a true story.

When I was 18 years old I went on a gap year to Tanzania in East Africa. I worked as a student teacher in a local school in Kilimanjaro, I had a wonderful time and it was the experience that convinced me to go into teaching. Personally I'm still rather surprised that any of our parents let us all go so far away from home to such a desperately poor area of the world. Anyway, they did and we were better for the experience. However, because we were a group of 18-year-olds in a remote place, there were some stupid occasions. One such experience was when six of us went on a safari together. We set up our camp for the night, and wandered over to the hippo pool that was there for visitors to watch from a distance.

So there we were, sitting on a bank several hundred yards away from the natural pool, watching three hippos as the sun set. It was charming. We ascertained that we were looking at a little family – mother, father and baby – with the baby hippo sitting on the mother hippo's head. So every few minutes the baby would pop up above the water's surface and then go up another few feet as her mother came up for air too. It was all very amusing and was excellent photo material.

Except Simon and I didn't have good cameras; they lacked any zoom feature.

So, largely because we were 18 and daft, Simon and I decided to venture down the bank for a slightly closer look. In fact, not only did we go to the water's edge, but we also walked along something of a natural jetty. Oh dear.

So Simon and I stood there, at the edge of the natural jetty, with our cameras at the ready, waiting for the shot we were both looking for. And, sure enough, mother and baby hippo popped up in the middle of the lake and we snapped away with our cameras. However, they still felt a little far away in our cameras' viewfinders, so we waited around to see if they would pop up a little closer.

Imagine two 18-year-old boys standing at the water's edge, poised with cameras to their faces, grinning and waiting. Sure enough, mother and baby appeared closer to us. Right in front of us. The mother stepped out of the water, her baby sliding down her back and into the water. She opened her mouth wide and roared at us, vaguely how you might expect a Tyrannosaurus Rex to sound.

We ran.

I ran faster than I had ever run.

I was quite unfit, but somehow I overtook first Simon and then the rest of the group! I travelled hundreds of yards in what felt like seconds, all to avoid certain death in the clutches of a large, smelly hippopotamus. The fear and terror of literally running for my life spurred me on like nothing ever had before or has since. I was superhuman, bounding across the plains of Africa in giant leaps to escape my enemy and claim victory for all humankind. It was a moment of potential glory versus potential gloom. Was I going to succeed? Was I going to survive? I looked behind me to see what carnage the hippo might be creating ...

Fortunately for us, the hippo was just scaring us off, and had not even got out of the water, let alone given chase. If it had decided to run, then there's a strong chance I would not be writing this book, as hippos run faster than humans. Even superhuman versions of me.

Not that I can normally run fast. After about ten yards I begin to feel tired, breathless and rather ashamed of myself. But at that moment I became superhuman, all because there was a mass of adrenalin pumping round my body. I'm sure you are familiar with the term *fight or flight*; well, that's what my story is an example of (and I promise it really is a true story) – my body reacted to the extreme situation with enough adrenalin to pump up my muscles ready either to run away from the hippo or to stay there and stand my ground. Like that would have worked.

The reason for this remarkable natural reaction is all to do with our species' primitive days when this 'fight or flight' response was employed daily against some very physical dangers. While going out to catch dinner, early humans had a lot to contend with and they were constantly fighting for their lives against beasts, the elements and each other. Adrenalin was put to good use, and when it got used it got used up, allowing the body to return to its normal non-superhuman self once the danger has passed.

So when you are faced with a physical stress, adrenalin is released into your bloodstream to give you energy and quick reaction speed. Your blood pressure also rises to force blood into your arms and legs ready to spring into action of some kind. Your heart rate speeds up and circulation to the brain and muscles increases at the expense of the digestive system. The lungs are stimulated for more oxygen and the liver releases sugar. All to get you in a state of readiness to catch dinner, defend your territory, or some other exciting primeval danger.

However, your body will react to any kind of stress in the same way. And most of the time in our modern world the stress we tend to experience is mental stress – that is to say stress caused by what we think. How stressed you get is generally dependent on how different your current situation is from the way you would like it to be.

Mental stress takes lots of forms – it can be about how we are going to fit everything in before all the deadlines hit, about how we are going to deal with that pupil who is always misbehaving, about all the problems we have in our home lives as well as our professional ones. They all cause adrenalin to start pumping its way around the body ready for you to face the physical challenge of catching dinner. Unfortunately your goal isn't to catch dinner, it's far more cerebral. And in teaching it can be a daily experience.

Tension in the muscles of your body is probably the most obvious response to your mental stress. You may not notice the tension within you, but this does not mean it is not there. Apart from ending up with crease lines on your forehead and face, a tight jaw, clenched fists, tension headaches, backache and a sore neck, tension affects your capacity to function effectively.

One way this can happen is through its effect on your diaphragm. The diaphragm controls your breathing and is particularly vulnerable to tension. A tense diaphragm leads to shallow breathing and consequently to a reduced flow of oxygen to the brain and an increase in certain chemicals in the blood which cause the brain to become sluggish.

Tension can also restrict the flow of blood to the brain, depriving it further of oxygen and nutrients. As a result, your capacity to concentrate, remember, listen and observe is reduced, making you a rather less useful version of yourself than you'd like to be. Which can, of course, cause you more mental stress.

There are fatty acids in your system which don't get burned up because you are not running for your life or catching dinner. Instead they attach themselves to the walls of your arteries and, along with the chemicals and other residue, silt up your body cells and inhibit their healthy function. Adrenalin hangs in the system and makes you jumpy, irritable, uptight and on edge. The body goes into a mild form of shock, and the mind becomes foggy and confused.

You can become preoccupied with the sorts of thoughts which cause stress. If you're preoccupied with these thoughts, you will find it very difficult also to focus properly on what you are reading, hearing, studying, marking, planning, teaching and so on. Have you ever put off doing something because you feel that it is too much hassle when you know that is not that difficult to do really?

So basically stress causes physiological problems that affect the way you think, preventing logic from playing any useful part in your mind's activities: your fears and your adrenalin will get the better of you.

Creative Teaching

Let's do a little test to see how stressed you are. I've listed below a whole load of stressful situations you might be in and given them a stress score out of 100. Tick all the situations that you feel you are in now, or have been in the last six months, or may well be in the next six months. They cover both common personal and professional circumstances. I've provided space for you to add some of your own stressful situations too. Total up the overall stress score; the higher it is, the higher your stress levels. If it comes to over 150, you are stressed – overly stressed. In any case, make sure you read the stress-reducing techniques that follow.

☐ Death of a close family member	100
☐ Death of a close friend	73
☐ Divorce	65
☐ Major personal injury/operation/etc.	63
☐ Getting married	58
☐ Buying a house	55
☐ End of serious long-term relationship	52
☐ Change in health of a family member	48
☐ Sex problems	46
☐ You are pregnant	44
☐ Your partner is pregnant	40

☐ Serious family arguments	39
☐ Second breadwinner loses job	38
☐ Dislike current job	37
☐ New boyfriend or girlfriend	36
☐ Difficulty with behaviour management	35
☐ Increased workload at school	35
☐ Outstanding personal achievement	34
☐ Harassment from a pupil	33
☐ Starting work at a new school	30
☐ Serious argument with senior staff	30
☐ Change in sleeping habits	29
☐ Change in social habits	29
☐ Change in eating habits	28
☐ Minor personal injury	26
☐ Minor traffic violation	20
☐ _____	__
☐ _____	__
☐ _____	__

Stress score   __

How did you do? You probably scored quite highly. As an anecdotal guide, this list is quite good because it is hard to quantify stress levels and this tool allows you to get some idea of just how much stress you could legitimately be feeling.

Personal management is essentially to be able to use your creative state successfully. Primary to that is being able to manage your stress levels: knowing your boundaries, recognizing when you've gone past those boundaries and being able to handle those situations. It's about being able to react from the head, instead of emotionally. Or, better still, to be able to predict the situation rather than react to it.

Dealing with stress

There are a number of ways to deal with stress, starting from a simple awareness strategy, and then on to ways to deal with stress as it happens, and finally more preventative measures you can take.

An awareness strategy

It's very hard to spot the moment you become stressed about something. It can take different forms: for example, anger towards a misbehaving pupil or a lack of focus caused by lots of deadlines. Two different situations, two different reactions, but one physiological response: stress and tension.

If you find yourself snapping a lot at your pupils, or showing other signs of stress, but you are unaware of the causes or when you start to show signs of stress, then you could try giving yourself a running commentary about your emotional state.

I'm feeling very tired,
pupil x is doing such-and-such,
it annoys me because ...
I want to shout at him and say ...

It's not a terribly natural thing to do, obviously, but try it for a day, or even an hour, to gauge how you react to situations. A running commentary requires you to be logical, so you might find yourself judging your reactions as you do them, or before you do them. This might stop you from doing something you might regret, from overreacting, or it may well justify your actions entirely. But at least you'll be more aware of what was causing your stress.

As far as facing workload issues such as marking and report writing, and the large pile of paperwork, consider first making sure you have prioritized everything. Simply write a list of everything that needs to be done and order it in terms of imminence and the time you estimate it will require. You could start by grading things A, B and C in terms of their importance, and then numbering them off in the order that you will approach them. This way you will have a much clearer idea as to why and when you should tackle certain bits of paperwork.

As for report writing, do not feel guilty about preparing several basic reports and then adapting the relevant report to a pupil. It gives you a valid framework to start from and can do a lot to remove the pressure of writing reports.

Dealing with stress as it happens

There are all sorts of possible scenarios here. You could be at home thinking about problems at work; you could be at school facing a pupil who is about to get the better of you; you could be feeling that you just can't be bothered; you could be feeling angry or upset; or it could all just be getting a bit too much for you. Whatever situation you find yourself in, here are a few simple ideas to deal with all that adrenalin and stress and be a bit better prepared to enter into your creative state.

Breathe properly. Stress will cause a tense diaphragm, which will in turn make your breathing shallow and your brain more sluggish. By taking control of your breathing you can relax the diaphragm muscles and stop stress from getting a tighter hold. Essentially you are preventing your more primitive, dinner-hunting, instincts from taking over by being properly self-aware.

Simply breathe in to the count of three, hold it for the count of three, and let it out slowly to the count of five. People vary about whether they prefer to do this through the mouth or nose. You should do as you please. The point here is to get rid of shallow breathing, filling up your lungs and relaxing tense muscles. You can also use this when you are having trouble getting to sleep. Instead of churning round lots of stressful thoughts in your mind, focus instead on breathing properly.

Another idea is to count to six every time you feel that you are about to snap at someone. In that time, your left brain will have had a chance to kick in and assess whether it is really worth your while getting stressed about the situation or whether there is a more peaceful solution. Seeing as stress is caused by your perception of the situation you are in or are thinking about, then it stands to reason that you can remove stress by assessing the situation more logically, accurately or positively. On what I would hope was an obvious note, this does not negate situations when a genuine stress response is needed: if a pack of wild dogs (or pupils) is chasing after you, then please don't try counting or looking at the positive side, just run and run fast!

Notice that there are two basic principles used here so far: the first strategy (breathing) deals with the physiological aspect of stress – that is to say, it deals with the effect it has on your body by doing an activity to dissipate it. The second strategy (counting to six) is basically mind over matter – it deals with the psychological aspect of stress and uses reason to tell the mind that it does not need to feel stressed. Be ready to apply these general principles when trying to deal with stress.

A more thorough method to deal with the physiological aspect of stress is to exercise. While mental stress does not elicit the need to fight or flee, your body is tensed up ready to do something physical. So do something physical if you can. Many schools allow teachers to use their sports facilities: pull some weights or go swimming; alternatively go for a jog or a brisk walk. Or you could do some exercises in your home such as press-ups, crunches, jogging on the spot, or even yoga. Yoga? Yes, yoga. Here are two exercises for you to try:

The eagle stretch

Stage 1 pose

- ◆ Stand with your feet together.

- ◆ Check your arms: which one is right and which is left, don't mix them up!

- ◆ Bring your right arm under your left arm, crossing at the elbow.

- ◆ Twist your right hand towards your face and around the left forearm.

- ◆ Place your right palm against the left palm, perfectly flat to each other, fingertips to fingertips.

- ◆ Keep your palms flat against each other and your chin up. Lower your shoulders and pull down your arms, bringing them towards your chest.

- ◆ Fit your mini-steeple nicely under your nose like an eagle's beak! This might be rather tricky at first, but you will get better at it I'm sure.

Stage 2 pose

Keep your feet together, spine straight, and your heels on the floor. Bend your knees about six inches until you feel a healthy pull. Look at a point in front of you and focus on it so that you don't fall over.

Now transfer your weight to your left leg and slowly lift your right leg up high. Bring your right leg over your left thigh and wrap your right leg's calf and foot around the lower part of your left leg. The top of your big toe should hook around the left leg's ankle.

Why?

The eagle stretch improves blood flow to the kidneys, helps firm calves, thighs, hips and abdomen muscles. It also increases blood flow to your brain, which improves concentration and alertness.

The awkward stretch

Stage 1 pose

- Stand with your feet about six inches apart, heels and toes nice and straight.

- Raise your arms in front of you, parallel with the floor, palms down, fingers together, arms and hands about six inches apart.

- Look at one point in front of you that is at eye level and keep focused on that point.

- Keep your heels flat on the floor and knees apart, sit down until the backs of your thighs are parallel with the floor and stop there. (Pretend there is a chair behind you and you are sitting on it.)

Creative Teaching

Stage 2 pose

Now arch your spine back, aiming for a perfectly straight spine, as though your back were against a wall. To do this, put your weight on your heels, raising your toes off the floor as you arch your back. Keep toes, heels, knees and hands all six inches apart, hold this pose to the count of ten.

Stage 3 pose

Slowly come up. Still keeping hands, arms and feet all six inches apart, and arms parallel to floor, stand up on your toes.

Why?

The awkward stretch increases blood circulation in knees and ankle joints. It strengthens and firms all muscles of the thighs, calves, hips and arms. And it gets your blood pumping, increasing the flow of blood to your brain.

It's all in the mind

So that's some physical strategies, what about some psychological ones? Well, by far and away the most popular one is visual imagery. Modern-day mental stress is caused by what you think, so think of something else. Select a scenario in your mind that makes you smile and relax, and then think of it whenever things are getting a bit too much. It might be a nice beach or other holiday spot where you felt relaxed. Or it could be a funny moment from a film, book or real life that just makes you smile. These ideas are designed to help you regain perspective, to stop you making a challenge become a threat or even a catastrophe. At the end of a bad lesson, when you can feel the stress getting to you, just ask yourself, 'Did the world end?' If it didn't, and nobody got injured, then congratulate yourself – it could have been much worse.

Long-term strategies

The best strategies for dealing with stress work when you combine the physical and psychological strategies. Any activity that combines mind and body will help you tremendously. Going out for the night with friends should be a great stress relief – you get the cathartic input from your friends and the physical exercise of dancing, walking, paintballing or whatever else you like to get up to at the weekend. I'm sure you'll be glad to have it confirmed that sex is an excellent form of stress relief, particularly when it is with someone special to you because of the psychological connection you have. Failing that, then meditation will work well, particularly in the form of something like T'ai Chi, which combines your thoughts and your actions into a peaceful state.

However you choose to relax, it is important to think of life as a process to go through. You tend to think that deadlines, pupils, paperwork, management, etc. cause you mental stress, but they don't. Your thoughts cause you stress: what you think about these things; how you evaluate them in your mind.

A common evaluation is to see consequences as 'horrible'. 'Horriblizing' the consequences of your behaviour is what causes most mental stress. The less stressful alternative is to think of these consequences as being 'unfortunate' (rather than horrible), and maybe even 'predictable'. The bottom line is that if you put whatever dedication and work is required into achieving a more creative classroom, then you'll probably get it. If you don't put in the work, or don't acquire the necessary skills and strategies, then there's not a lot of sense worrying about the predictable outcome.

Entering your creative state

So in order to be successfully creative you need to be calm. Not so calm that you have become docile – you need to remain alert and on the ball – just calm enough to accept that your pupils might be noisier, might be out of their seats, might have to work together, might not do any writing, or whatever other things you have planned for the lesson (more about that later). You need to be prepared to manage such situations calmly, and with good, positive, behaviour-management strategies in place. As soon as you show agitation, you suggest to pupils that you are not in control of yourself or the class, and this can become an opportunity for less motivated pupils to sabotage your efforts.

Self-talk is a good place to start. As you walk to your classroom, tell yourself something to get yourself motivated. I suggest it's something that makes you smile. Tell yourself that you're fab, that you are a creative genius, a mastermind of your subject (which is, of course, the best subject in the world) and the epitome of calm, emotional stability in a world of never-ending possibilities. Got the idea?!

It also helps if you visualize your class, how you are going to address them and what activities you are going to do with them. Tell yourself (and them) that you think they are all marvellous (even if they are not), and think of calm, non-confrontational ways you can

33

anticipate and prevent bad behaviour. More advice on dealing with behaviour can be found in Sue Cowley's excellent *Getting the Buggers to Behave* (Continuum).

Of course, this mental preparation is only any use if you have something to put into practice with your pupils. There are certain fundamental educational theories about creativity and pupils that you need to know about and employ in your teaching. In themselves they should help you feel creative. Below I will outline more about how the brain learns and I will explain three major theories. Later in the book I will give you practical advice about applying these theories in your classroom and in your school. By theories, I refer to the more scientific use of the word: a valid concept that has been tested and has considerable proof that supports it, and is still open to further investigation and proof, but is no longer seriously open to being disproved or disregarded. Like the big bang theory, for instance.

Creativity and learning

Learning is not something that happens to pupils. They are not passive vessels to be filled up with information. They are not sponges that soak up every word you utter. They might have been when younger, but at secondary school they become selective. Their RAS has kicked in and will discard information or activity that does not get their attention – the same as you would. As they grow up they want to be treated more like adults, and that means they also need to take responsibility for their actions.

As teachers we are quick to apply this rule to their behaviour, but what about their learning behaviour? Surely if we expect them to act responsibly in the classroom, then we should expect them to learn with a sense of responsibility too? Nurturing a sense of ownership of and self-development through their work is a crucial part of creative learning. Without doing so, pupils will continue to be passive creatures and will never develop the level of autonomy and improved learning performance of which they are capable.

Knowing how to learn can unlock all sorts of possibilities in pupils. If they learn the study skills of how the brain processes information, how they can participate more actively in the learning process, what their preferred learning styles are, and how to revise effectively, then they can be empowered to take more interest in and responsibility for their work and there can be real improvement in pupils' learning performance.

We've already touched on a bit about the reticular activating system (RAS) and the right (creative) and left (logical) parts of the brain. But how does the brain actually learn?

Creative Teaching

Neural pathways

A neuron is a brain cell that we can use to store and process information (that is to say, we think using cells called neurons). One neuron connects with other neurons and forms a tiny electrical current between those cells, a neural pathway. It is fair (if not completely accurate) to say that this neural pathway represents a piece of information, a concept, an idea, etc. that you have learned.

The more things you learn, the more neural pathways you form in your mind. These pathways link up with other related pathways and as a result you will develop a better understanding of the material you are learning about, and you'll be able to form opinions and insights about it.

In order to memorize that information, you need to reinforce it by reviewing it now and again. Doing this makes that neural pathway light up in your brain and become stronger. The more times you light up those neural pathways, the quicker your brain will find the information and the longer it will stay accessible to your memory.

At this point I could start talking in more detailed technical terms, mentioning axons, dendrites and synapses. But I'm sure that you don't have all day to read about this. Suffice it to say that an axon is the neuron's transmitter and dendrites are a neuron's

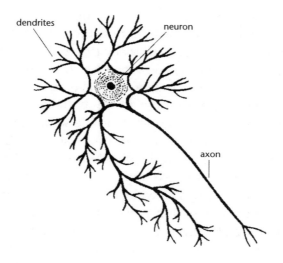

receptors. The synaptic cleft is the tiny gap formed between connecting axons and dendrites that allows the electrical signal (otherwise known as a thought) to go from the connecting neuron to the receiving neuron. A single neuron can receive signals from thousands of other neurons all at once. That neuron may then transmit an electrical signal to thousands of other neurons and the process of thinking takes place.

Our brains are, by and large, the same. They all have about the same number of brain cells as each other, so good news: you have something in common with Einstein after all. And so do all your pupils. You see, it's not the number of brain cells that is important, it's the number of connections you make between them that counts. You may well have more neurons than there are stars in the Milky Way (you really do), but if you're not using them effectively, you won't be so bright!

Einstein made more than the average number of neural connections in order to be as clever as he was, and we all have the potential to do the same. Obviously, the connections you make are often affected by your experiences, particularly in childhood, and the more pathways that are formed and strengthened early on in life, the better. Likewise, what you eat, how much you sleep, and the perceptions you hold are all contributory factors to the effectiveness of your neural network.

It is fair to say that the make-up of each individual's brain is unique. Your brain consists of a range of faculties that are reasonably separate from each other – they certainly occupy different areas of the brain – and have developed depending on the stimuli they have received. Such faculties include things like speaking, comprehending, reading, writing, spatial orientation, singing, and being able to relate to people. In people who have suffered damage to certain parts of their brain only certain faculties are disrupted and others continue to function normally. Your brain is not really one entity; it is a series of abilities that form connections to work together according to your experiences, your genes and your environment.

These connections and these abilities are not static, they can always be made better or worse, and as such there is a gap to be bridged between a student's current learning performance and his or her potential learning performance. Our goal as teachers is to stimulate and activate those neurons and those abilities. Of course you can't force a student to make and then strengthen neural connections, but you can motivate students to do so themselves.

VAK

We all learn by seeing, hearing and doing. In more formal language, we all learn through our visual, auditory and kinaesthetic channels. These channels can work together – however, most people are likely to prefer one channel to the other two; this is referred to as your preferred learning channel or style. There are reasonably straightforward tests available to help students determine their preferred learning channel.

Research shows that there is a fairly even three-way split between people's channel preferences. A study of 5,300 students by Specific Diagnostic Studies Inc. of Rockville, Maryland, revealed that in any class in any subject in any school there tends to be on average:

◆ 29 per cent students with a visual preference

♦ 34 per cent students with a auditory preference

♦ 37 per cent students with a kinaesthetic preference

Essentially, the evidence from the last 30 years of research in this area (Bandler and Grinder* developed this concept as part of their Neuro-Linguistic Programming project in the 1970s) suggests that those students of yours who insist on rocking on the back legs of their chairs and flicking bits of paper across the room would actually take part in your lessons and learn if they were able to participate in an active, kinaesthetic way.

Don't panic, we're not about to suggest that all teachers have to start competing with the Art or PE departments for the messiest/most active classroom in the school; there are plenty of simple and easy ways to incorporate kinaesthesia in teaching and learning. The impact of feeling excluded from learning, by not being 'clever' enough to understand academic (visual–auditory) teaching and learning, cannot be underestimated.

You probably have plenty of visual and auditory activities in your lessons. Visual activities like reading, drawing and writing are extremely valid learning tools. Auditory activities like giving a talk, listening to you and each other, are again extremely useful skills. You also

* Bandler, R., Grinder, J. *et al.* (1981), *Frogs into Princes: Neuro-Linguistic Programming*. Moab, UT: Real People Press.

get television documentaries and PowerPoint presentations which combine visual and auditory channels – again, great. I'm not suggesting for one minute that any of these activities should be discarded – after all, we all learn through all three learning channels.

However, there is much to be said for incorporating the kinaesthetic. Some activities are wholly kinaesthetic – like doing actions to keywords or ideas to remember, or creating role-plays or a tableau of an event. Others neatly combine with the other two styles: a discussion where pupils have to move around the room from one person to another; or a creative writing exercise where the pupil has to imagine him- or herself in a given situation. The best kinaesthetic activities involve the pupil as directly as possible in the content to be learned – it gives them a relevant context, a hook, a handle, to comprehend and learn.

Fact box 2: Preferred learning styles and teaching

Your own preferred learning style will affect your teaching style. Teachers with an auditory preference tend to do a lot more talking to (or rather, at) the class than more visual or kinaesthetic teachers. Teachers with a kinaesthetic preference are easy to spot: they are the teachers who sit on their desks and don't mind a bit of noise from their class. Teachers with a visual preference are far more likely than their other colleagues to have lots of bright, colourful displays on their walls.

Of course, learning preferences are not fixed, nor are they an exact science. You can take a quiz to see where your preferences might lie, and this will give you a good indication, but you will know best yourself when you reflect on how you conduct yourself in the classroom – what do you prefer doing?

Here's a preferred learning styles quiz to take. Tick or highlight your most likely reaction to each situation. Try to avoid ticking more than one – you are looking to assess your first response to a situation, not all of your responses! Then count up the number of Vs, As and Ks your scored. The one with the highest score is your most preferred learning style, followed by your second and then your least preferred style.

What do you notice most about people?
V how they look or dress?
A how they sound when they talk?
K how they stand or move?

How do you learn most easily?
V by reading and observing?
A by being told what to do?
K by getting stuck in and doing it for yourself?

If you had to wait for a bus, would you probably:
V watch and admire the scenery, or read?
A talk to or phone people?
K walk around and fidget?

What would make you think someone was lying?
  V the way they look, or avoid looking, at you?
  A their tone of voice?
  K a feeling you get about their sincerity?

When you have many things to do, do you:
  V make lists for yourself?
  A keep reminding yourself you have things to do?
  K feel restless until all or most of the things are done?

What kind of humour do you prefer?
  V cartoons/comics?
  A stand-up comedians?
  K slapstick?

At a party do you tend to spend most of your time:
  V watching what is happening?
  A talking and listening to others?
  K circulating around or dancing?

When you are learning, do you prefer:
  V work that is written and drawn in colour?
  A to listen to a talk or be told what to do?
  K to be active: making and doing?

You solve problems most easily by:
  V writing or drawing out possible solutions
  A talking through possible solutions
  K getting stuck in and working it out as you go

Creative Teaching

When you are angry, do you:
- V   silently seethe inside?
- A   shout and scream?
- K   clench your fists, grit your teeth, stomp about and go away angry?

Your preferred/favourite way to relax is:
- V   watch TV or read
- A   listen to the radio/music
- K   do a physical activity (e.g. playing sport)

When trying to remember people, do you tend to:
- V   remember faces, but forget names?
- A   remember names, but forget faces?
- K   remember things I did with them?

In a video shop you are more likely to rent:
- V   action adventure
- A   musicals
- K   dramas

You try to spell a new or difficult word by:
- V   writing it to see how it looks
- A   sounding it out
- K   writing it to see how it feels

Total number of Vs   _____

Total number of As   _____

Total number of Ks   _____

Multiple intelligences

Earlier I mentioned that the brain is a series of fairly separate faculties that work together. Howard Gardner famously developed his theory of Multiple Intelligences in line with this thinking. Essentially Gardner* defines intelligence as an ability or potential to solve problems or create something in a way that is beneficial (in whatever context one is in – from the classroom to the whole world).

Having noticed that people seem to be clever in different ways – just compare Mozart to Newton – he went about assessing ways in which people could be intelligent. He used a set of eight testable criteria, which included things like psychological tasks and questions like *does it have a dedicated area of the brain?* He originally concluded that there were seven intelligences, and has since appended an eighth.

First you have your academic intelligences: *linguistic intelligence*, which involves spoken and written language and its use and is the province of lawyers, speakers, writers, poets, translators and the like; and *logical–mathematical intelligence*, which involves being able to analyse problems logically and is the domain of mathematicians, logicians and scientists.

* Gardner, H. (1999), *Intelligence Reframed: Multiple Intelligences for the 21st Century.* New York: Basic Books.

Creative Teaching

Next there are the more artistic intelligences. *Musical intelligence* deals with areas such as performance, composition and appreciation of musical patterns. Gardner noted that the patterns of understanding music are very similar to that of language, and therefore sees no reason why he should regard the latter as an intelligence and the former as a talent. *Bodily kinaesthetic intelligence* refers to those who use their bodies to solve problems or create things, such as dancers, actors, athletes, craftsmen, surgeons and mechanics. *Spatial intelligence* is about the ability to recognize and manipulate patterns of space, whether they be small (think sculptors and surgeons) or big (think aeroplane pilots).

Then there are the personal intelligences: *interpersonal* and *intrapersonal*. Interpersonal intelligence is the ability to understand people's intentions, motivations and desires and/or to be able to work with them. Salespeople, teachers, actors, religious leaders and political leaders are all good examples of people who possess interpersonal intelligence. *Intrapersonal intelligence* refers to your ability to know and understand yourself, your desires, fears and capacities and is measured not by people's jobs and activities, but by how well you can regulate your own life.

Gardner endorsed an eighth intelligence (and is happy for there to be more, provided that they meet his criteria). This eighth intelligence is the *naturalist intelligence*, demonstrated by how well one understands the patterns of the physical world, recognizes species and spots relations, and/or is able to care for, tame or interact with living creatures. Hunters, fishermen, farmers, gardeners, cooks, biologists and of course naturalists all exhibit naturalist intelligence.

Gardner has also been tempted to add a ninth intelligence, the *existential intelligence*, which would deal with one's ability to appreciate and tackle the big questions of existence, but there is not quite enough proof that this ability merits separate treatment from the other eight intelligences. A good existential philosopher would draw on their naturalist, linguistic, interpersonal and intrapersonal intelligences.

Bear in mind that each intelligence will have different end results in different people: I might have musical intelligence, but that doesn't make me Mozart. Wayne Sleep might have bodily kinaesthetic intelligence, but that doesn't mean he would be any good as a surgeon. Each intelligence is something of an umbrella term for a range of subintelligences which, when nurtured and combined with other subintelligences, will form a unique neural circuitry that will make that person good at whatever they are good at.

The point of knowing about this in the creative teaching context is that you can, of course, tap into pupils' intelligences better to engage with them and help them learn. Using narratives is good for linguistic intelligence; using deductive reasoning helps with logical–mathematical intelligence, as does denoting the connections between items of information your pupils are learning; using art, music and other things aesthetic helps with the arts-based intelligences; doing something hands-on, such as visiting a museum or performing experiments, is good for bodily kinaesthetic intelligence and doing something social like group-based discovery tasks is good for both personal intelligences.

However, you should be slightly wary about testing pupils to find their multiple intelligences and then labelling them accordingly. By all means test your pupils to find out which intelligences they have strengths in, but do so in an intelligence-specific way. Most MI tests available are tickbox pencil-and-pen tests, which by their nature are linguistic and logical–mathematical, and are therefore not accurate measuring tools for all the other intelligences. To measure someone's musical intelligence, see how well they can recognize or sing a tune; to measure someone's spatial intelligence, see how they perform on a Duke of Edinburgh Scheme field trip.

It is also unwise to try to quantify how intelligent someone is in each area – for example, to say that you are 35 per cent interpersonally intelligent, 25 per cent linguistically intelligent and so on. Multiple intelligences are not static, particularly among your pupils, and they will change as pupils make progress. It should be suffi-cient to identify ability in areas and give support in the development of that intelligence, as well as improve weaker areas too.

Neither is it necessary to teach the same thing in eight different ways to suit each intelligence. It is both unnecessary and impractical. But the more angles you can give to learning a topic, then the more likely pupils will understand and memorize it. So the creative teacher needs to think of what intelligences can be drawn upon appropriately to help pupils learn a given topic. And once you've taught it, you need to evaluate how it went and what could be improved next time around. It is not as though failing to teach something via a particular learning style equates with a pupil's failure to learn. Everyone learns in a multitude of ways, and multiple intelligences provide a good checklist to use to ensure that you are using a range of engaging methods.

More ideally, learning is personalized to each of your pupils. Imagine if your school had completed an appropriate MI test, and a VAK test, and you knew your pupils' learning strengths and weaknesses. You could then set different forms of learning activities to pupils to play to their strengths or improve weaker areas as appropriate. Marvellous. But the reality is that this is too big an ask of teachers, it requires time and resources beyond our current education system. And to be applied properly, the national curriculum would have to, at least, become a lot more flexible to allow pupils to excel in subjects more appropriate to their intellectual abilities. Not likely. But when opportunities arise to get to know your pupils' personalities, then take it and ask them about what they enjoy doing. It might give you some insight into their intelligences and what learning methods might be appropriate to them, and give you some ideas for activities to do with your class or with that pupil when they seem to be struggling.

VAK and Multiple Intelligences are complementary, not conflicting, theories. Think of VAK as a different perspective on what happens in your classroom. You might prefer to think in terms of VAK when planning a lesson or a scheme of work, or you might prefer to think in terms of MI, or both. As long as there is variety in approach, then pupils will be better engaged and have more opportunities to get to grips with your subject. Both of these theories provide you with resources and frameworks to create that variety; it all comes down to personal preference.

Emotional intelligence

The third and final theory I would like to look at here is Emotional Intelligence. It is not linked directly with Multiple Intelligences, but it does focus upon your interpersonal and intrapersonal intelligences. It is appropriate here because it encapsulates something about your psyche and that of the pupils and colleagues you know. Developed by two psychologists from the USA, Salovey and Mayer*, it has become something of a well-established concept in both business and education. Emotional Intelligence, or EI or EQ, is to do with your ability to perceive, understand and express your feelings accurately and to control your emotions so that they work for you and not against you. It is all about self-awareness and empathy.

This is important in creative teaching on two counts: for your own EI and to develop your pupils' EI. Schools that aim to develop their pupils' emotional and social awareness will focus, among other things, on enabling pupils to recognize their emotional states, developing empathy by identifying non-verbal clues as to how someone feels, managing stress, understanding what motivates and demotivates them, improving listening skills and learning and applying conflict resolution strategies. The University of Illinois at Chicago tested schools committed to teaching such strategies and demonstrated that 50 per cent of pupils improved academically, misbehaviour dropped by an average of 28 per cent, and exclusions by 44 per cent. 63 per cent of pupils demonstrated considerably more positive behaviour. All of this was attributed to the success of their EI projects.

* Mayer, J. D., Salovey, P. and Brackett, M. A. (2004), *Emotional Intelligence: Key Readings on the Mayer and Salovey Model*. New York: DUDE Publishing.

Creative Teaching

EI should not be mistaken for a revolutionary new concept. It enshrines something in scientific terms that resonates with religious beliefs, philosophy and society throughout time. Aristotle once said that *anyone can become angry – that is easy. But to be angry with the right person, to the right degree, at the right time, for the right purpose, and in the right way – that is not easy* (*Nicomachean Ethics*). Aristotle's point here is that our feelings often get in the way; they seem to hijack thoughts and reactions from the more intellectual areas of our brain and replace them with thoughts and reactions from our lower brain functions instead. When you should react with sympathy and solutions, you go into 'fight or flight' mode.

As a creative teacher it is important that you have a high EQ (as opposed to IQ) so that you can manage yourself effectively. Being thoroughly self-aware and in control of yourself will make the difference between a safe, creative and empowering environment and a weak, messy and menacing one.

In summary

In order to be creative in the classroom you need to enter your creative state. It all comes down to knowledge and attitude. It is important to make sure that you understand the relevant educational theory properly; maybe even just reading this section has given you one or two ideas for doing something creative in your classroom. With your knowledge up to speed, check your attitude. How stressed are you? How motivated are you? How emotionally intelligent do you feel? Develop the ideas given here and look into others if you need to.

Whenever you come to school, or prepare work for school, then get into your creative state. Just tell yourself that you are feeling motivated, that you are fabulous at your job (of course) and think positively; visualize your lessons going smoothly and enjoyably. I have given you some tips for managing stress levels associated with teaching; make sure you try some of them out. As soon as you let negativity creep in, then thinking creatively is just not going to happen because you will start thinking of all the pitfalls that *could* happen. You would be horriblizing potentially excellent experiences for both you and your pupils. So start your teaching day positively, develop a mantra if you need to.

The other thing you must do is to employ some of the learning styles information as soon as you can – even if you just make some notes about VAK and MI. Or, better still, analyse what you do at the moment to see where you are suitably meeting learning styles and where there are some areas you could develop. As soon

Creative Teaching

as you start using the ideas in this book, the sooner you will feel more creative.

The best technique to enter your creative state is the simplest – be yourself. Or rather, be the best possible version of yourself you can be.

2 The creative classroom

What do pupils need in order to learn creatively?

So, we have looked at fundamental educational theory, and looked at how you can prepare your mindset in a positive way to approach creative teaching. But what about your pupils? What do they need, specifically?

I feel that in order to engage with creative learning and improve their learning performance, pupils need:

- knowledge of how to learn and a sense of self-responsibility
- clear structure in their learning
- reasons to be interested in your subject

Creative Teaching

- a positive rapport with their teachers
- appropriate stimuli to keep the RAS alert
- positive and constructive feedback

Why?

Knowledge of how to learn and a sense of self-responsibility

As stated in the last section, learning is not something that happens to a pupil. It is something in which they need to participate. Doing so can have a remarkable impact on a child's attitude not only to learning, but also to their life beyond and after school. Knowing how their brain works and what they can do to help themselves learn is the key to creative learning. They realize that there is an active role for them to play in their education, and they will become more involved in your lessons. This can be nurtured and a sense of personal responsibility and ownership over their learning can be developed. Doing this leads to all sorts of creative possibilities in their learning, but at a fundamental level it gets them on your side and interested in learning.

Clear structure in their learning

It is no good appealing to pupils' right brain and getting all creative, if you don't level that out with structure from the left brain. Information is inherently logical, but it can be presented as a series of unconnected ideas. Teachers need to ensure that they are being as logical as possible, organizing information in a clear structure to make sure it makes sense. Likewise, pupils need to have a sense of how their learning activities at one moment fit in with other learning activities. They need to see a 'big picture' of the information they are learning. So creative teaching requires a systematic approach to learning.

Similarly, if pupils perceive your creative lessons as a series of daft games with little or no relevance to anything they are learning, then the whole process becomes pointless, and probably rather rowdy too. Pupils need to understand why they are doing what they are doing, and the consequences of not following instructions. For example, can you trust your pupils to discuss something in pairs without starting to chat about last night's TV instead? A strong discipline structure based on trust and personal responsibility on the part of the pupil forms the backbone of any successful creative classroom. See 'A note about discipline' (below) for more about creative environments and discipline.

Creative Teaching

A note about discipline

This is a tricky one. You need to give pupils enough leeway to express themselves creatively, but maintain enough control to make sure that pupils don't abuse this level of freedom. 'Strict and scary' styles of teaching don't lend themselves to a successful creative environment, but neither does the Joyce Grenfell approach. It's about mixing approachability and authority, being clear about what you want, being fair and having high expectations. There are plenty of good books out there about discipline, so I won't attempt a thorough investigation of it here as I won't be able to do it justice. Suffice it to say you need to have clear ground rules about attempts to sabotage an activity or failing to participate. When warning a pupil about their behaviour, you need to be clear as to *why* the pupil's behaviour is wrong, how they should remedy the situation and what consequences they may face if their behaviour remains unacceptable. You need to be firm and consistent without being confrontational or aggressive. Most or all your complaint is directed towards the pupil's behaviour, not their personality, and the consequence is a result of their behaviour, not a punishment from you. This way you depersonalize the error and the sanction, meaning that neither you nor the pupil needs to lose face.

And if you don't know who Joyce Grenfell is, read her monologue that follows and use it as a guide as to what not to do when managing behaviour!

Nursery School – Going Home Time
a monologue by Joyce Grenfell

Children – it's time to go home, so finish tidying up and put on your hats and coats. Some of our mummies are here for us, so hurry up.

Billy won't be long, Mrs Binton. He's on hamster duty.

Now let's see if we can't all help each other. Janey – I said help each other. Help Bobbie carry that chair, don't pin him against the wall with it.

We're having a go at our good neighbour policy here, Mrs Binton, but it doesn't always ...

Neville, off the floor, please. Don't lie there.

And Sidney, stop painting, please.

Because it's time to go home.

Well, you shouldn't have started another picture, should you. What is it this time?

Another blue man! Oh, I see, so it is.

All right, you can make it just a little bit bluer, but only one more brushful, please, Sidney.

We don't think he's very talented, but we feel it's important to encourage their self-expression. You never know where it might lead ...

Rachel. Gently – help Teddy *gently* into his coat.

It's a lovely coat, Teddy, what's wrong with it?

Oh. It looks like a boy's coat when you wear it. And lots of boys wear pink.

Poor wee mite, he has three older sisters!

Neville, I said get up off the floor.

Who shot you dead?

David did? Well, I don't suppose he meant to. He may

have meant to then, but he doesn't mean it now, and anyhow I say you can get up.

No, don't go and shoot David dead, because it's time to go home.

George. What did I tell you not to do? Well, don't do it.

And Sidney, don't wave that paintbrush about like that, you'll splash somebody. LOOK OUT, DOLORES!

Sidney! ... It's all right, Dolores, you aren't hurt, you're just surprised. It was only a nice soft brush. But you'd better go and wash your face before you go home.

Because it's all blue.

Sidney, I saw you deliberately put that paintbrush up Dolores's little nostril.

No, it wasn't a jolly good shot. It ... I don't want to discuss it, Sidney.

Now go and tell Dolores you're sorry.

Yes, now.

Thank you, Hazel, for putting the chairs straight for me.

You are a great helper.

Thank you.

And thank you, Dicky, for closing the cupboard door for me.

Dicky ... is there somebody *in* the cupboard?

Well, let her out at once.

Are you all right, Peggy? What did you go into the cupboard for?

But we don't have mices – I mean mouses – in our toy cupboard. Mouses only go where there is food, and we don't have any food in our toy cupboard.

When did you hide a bicky in there?
Every day!
Well, perhaps we have got mices in our toy cupboard.
I'll have to look.
No, you go and get your coat on.
Dicky – We never shut people in cupboards.
Because they don't like it.
What do you mean, she's puggy? Peggy's puggy?
Oh, she's got puggy hands. But you don't have to hold her hand ...
Well, you must ask her nicely to let go.
Well, if she won't let go ...
You'll have to work it out for yourself, Dicky.
Edgar and Timmy ... your knitted caps are not for playing tug-of-war with. Look, now the pom-pom's come off.
Whose is it?
Well, give it back to Sidney.
Where are your caps?
Well, go and ask Sidney to give them back to you.
Turn round, Geoffrey. You've got your wellingtons on the wrong feet.
Yes, you have. You'll have to take them off and start again.
Why can't you reach?
Well, undo your coat and then you can bend.
Take off your woolly gloves.
And your scarf.
You can keep your balaclava on. How many jerseys are you wearing?
Heavens. No wonder you can't bend.
Caroline, come and help Geoffrey.

Don't kick her, Geoffrey. She's come to help.

Sidney, I told you to put that paintbrush down ... LOOK OUT, DOLORES!

Well, that wasn't a very good shot, was it? You didn't mean to put it in her ear, did you?

Well, you shouldn't have.

You're all right, Dolores. It was just a bit of a surprise, but you'll have to go and wash again.

Because you've got a blue ear.

Sidney, I'm ashamed of you, a big boy of four, and she's only just three.

And Sidney, what have you done with Timmy and Edgar's caps?

No, I'm not going to guess.

And I don't want to know they are hidden in a special secret place, I want to know exactly where they are.

No, I'm not going to try and find them. You're going to tell me where they are.

Well, go and get them out of the waste-paper basket at once. Waste-paper baskets aren't for putting caps in.

Now go and say you are sorry to Dolores.

Yes, again.

We think his aggression is diminishing, but we do have setbacks.

Lavinia, is that your coat you've got on? It looks so enormous.

Oh, you're going to grow into it. I see.

Hazel, thank you for helping Betty into her jacket.

Just zip her up once. Not up and down.

No, Neville, you can't have a turn.

No, children, you can't all zip Betty.

Jenny, come here.

Jenny, when we have paid a visit to the littlest room, what do we do?

We pull our knickers up again.

Good-bye, Hazel, Good-bye, Bobbie. Good-bye, everybody.

Good-bye, Mrs Binton.

Hurry up, Sidney, because you'll keep your Mummy waiting.

Well, your Granny then.

Somebody is coming to take you away, aren't they, Sidney?

Good.

No, you won't see me tomorrow, Sidney.

Tomorrow is Saturday ... thank heaven.

Reasons to be interested in your subject

A very natural question that pupils ask themselves about anything they learn is 'What's in it for me?' This question is often not answered satisfactorily by the standard carrot of good exam grades. Pupils want to know why they should bother learning the things you have to teach them – what intrinsic value do they have? What relevance does this lesson have in the grand scheme of life?!

If a pupil is naturally motivated by your subject, then the intrinsic value of anything you teach them is obvious: they like your subject, want to know more and want to get better at it. But if they are not naturally interested in your subject, then the intrinsic value is less obvious. A pupil's RAS may not engage with your lessons and any work you give them, however creative you might make it, is 'pointless' or 'a waste of time'.

Often there are key skills to be gained from learning about a particular topic, or participating in a particular learning activity, and it is this kind of thing you need to emphasize to such pupils. If you can find ways of relating what you are teaching to something they are already familiar with in their own lives, then that can be a very powerful way in to pupils' interest. For instance, in modern foreign languages, you could show extracts from episodes of *Friends* or *The Simpsons* in your target language – they are available on DVD from the Amazon website of your target language's country. Even being able to say 'It's kind of like when …' and relating what you are learning about to something that they would have experienced before in real life or in a film or on television. Knowledge and understanding is, after all, based on associations you make between things you already know and the things you learn. If there isn't something familiar for your pupils to link new information to, then it loses context for them and is far harder to memorize or understand.

The creative classroom

A positive rapport with their teachers

This ties together the last three points. The rapport a teacher has with his or her pupils can make a huge difference; and it can largely be controlled by the teacher. Do they feel comfortable with you? The respect they have of you, is it out of fear or genuine respect for you and what you stand for? A positive attitude from the teacher makes a big difference to pupil motivation, behaviour and performance. But the teacher's attitude should also be conditional, the teacher should be very clear about the rules and what is and isn't acceptable and should take steps to demonstrate to pupils that misbehaviour (which includes a lack of effort or participation) is unacceptable.

The effect of making pupils feel valued (such as knowing their names, and something of their personality) cannot be underestimated. *Even if the teacher doesn't actually remember everybody's names, or care too much about the individual – or even like them!* The trick here is to make pupils feel as if what they are learning is important and relevant (so they understand why they are learning it), and make them care about the work – to get them feeling involved in the learning process. Once this is established, pupils will become more autonomous as they get older, and will be much more likely to enjoy learning for the sake of learning.

Creative Teaching

A teacher who does not appear to value or respect his or her pupils is unlikely to elicit such positive progress. However, if this is your teaching style (you're a 'strict and scary' teacher) and you wish to change tactics, then please don't just walk into class and act differently, valuing your pupils and being all positive and friendly. The pupils will think you've flipped and it won't work. I've included in this book some incremental steps to take that might work for you.

Appropriate stimuli to keep the RAS alert

Telling jokes, making the pupils feel welcome, using artefacts, questioning pupils, through to doing something more unusual like re-enactments, making models, or even just getting pupils to bob up in their seats instead of putting their hands up. These are all examples of creative stimuli that get pupils' attention.

Often creative teaching taps into the various learning styles models. Phil Beadle, 2004's Teacher of the Year, often sang silly songs to his pupils to tap into their musical intelligence. Maybe that's not what you're good at doing, but it is a legitimate example of creative stimuli that involve pupils in learning.

Positive and constructive feedback

How would you like it if at the end of a rather good lesson of yours, your pupils came up to you and said *'Very good work, but you need to pay more attention to the accuracy of your delivery. You did not ask Jack to answer any of your questions, even though his hand was up more often than not. You also failed to enquire how your pupils were at the start of the lesson and state the lesson objectives clearly. However, we did enjoy your lesson and we'll look forward to an even better one next time.'*

Imagine that you worked hard to prepare that lesson. You spent a lot of energy and care over getting it right, and you were happy that you had produced a very good lesson. Comments like the one above focus too heavily on what went wrong, and not enough on what went right and what to do about the things that went wrong. They are deflating despite the positive comments.

How many of us teachers are guilty of taking a good piece of work and spending more time criticizing it negatively than positively, contaminating the praise with a somewhat disproportionate list of errors without a similar list of good points? Creative teachers are meant to educate and inspire their pupils, not bombard them with a list of their failings with no constructive help on how to improve.

Creative Teaching

You and I know that marking and giving feedback involves looking for progress and development in their work, but in the context of my example above does it not seem a little terse? At least the pupils in my example gave prompt feedback; in our modern world of computer games and mobile phones, most feedback young people experience is fairly instant. In the classroom, for incredibly legitimate reasons, feedback can take a week (or more) to reach the pupil. Not terribly twenty-first-century, is it?!

As a teacher you need to look at the simplest solution to giving effective feedback. One simple piece of advice is to write/say 'and' wherever you might normally use 'but' to stop the 'negative' outweighing the positives. Another is to force yourself into a ratio of two positive comments to one constructive comment.

To speed things up, you could simply get pupils to identify their own targets and get them to do a self-assessment or peer-assessment about how effectively they met their targets. This could be an initial exercise prior to your final marking (which could focus solely on their targets if you wish) but at least there's some prompt feedback, and you are encouraging self-reflection which is an important tool that encourages and enables independent learning.

What teachers need to form a creative classroom

Getting into your creative state is very important. But there is a little more to it than just positive thinking and some knowledge about educational theory. Here are a few more things to consider:

♦ your willingness to self-evaluate

♦ your ability to develop, or change, what you do presently

♦ incorporating accelerated learning techniques and structures into lessons

♦ knowledge of how to teach creatively

♦ ideas to get started with

Willingness to self-evaluate

If you don't review what you do, then how can you ever assess if you can do better? Every job involves some self-evaluation, and teaching is no different. You probably do it quite naturally in your head – deciding if a lesson went well or not, and why, for example. But what about you as a teacher overall? When was the last time you reflected about how you conduct yourself as a teacher?

As you have read this far into the book, you are most probably willing and open-minded enough to do a little self-evaluation. You need to reflect on what you are doing at present to work out what you already do well, and what you might need to improve on or do differently. There is also some groundwork to be done in order to ensure that your classroom environment facilitates and encourages creativity. Use the classroom audit in the next fact box to assess how conducive your classroom environment is to a creative atmosphere.

Fact box 3: Classroom audit

The environment can have a very significant effect on students and staff alike. How someone feels about the environment around them has implications for how they behave in that environment. Take a look at the classroom you are in now and consider these points:

Outside of the classroom –
What is there around the door to the classroom to make the room inviting?

_____

_____

Describe the displays (if any) in the vicinity of the classroom.

_____

_____

How old do they appear to be?!

_____

Inside the classroom –

Displays

Describe the displays (if any) in the classroom.

_____

_____

Are the walls used effectively to encourage interest in the subject? For example: are there puzzles, things to debate, something interactive to use in a lesson, something to aid reviewing, something to promote the subject/topic?

Yes/No

Why? _____

_____

There are plants in the room   Yes/No
The classroom is tidy and well organized   Yes/No
The room is a pleasant environment to be in   Yes/No

What could you, the teacher, do to improve the environment of this classroom?

_____

_____

Maintenance

The walls and ceiling are clean and well painted	Yes/No
The tables are in good condition overall	Yes/No
The chairs are in good condition overall	Yes/No
The teacher's desk and chair is in good condition	Yes/No
The floors are carpeted	Yes/No
The classroom is tidy	Yes/No
The room is well ventilated	Yes/No
There are good-quality curtains or blinds at the windows	Yes/No
All the lights work	Yes/No

What could the school do to improve the environment of this classroom?

_____

_____

Equipment

There is a computer in the room	Yes/No
It shows signs of being used by the teacher	Yes/No
It is gathering dust	Yes/No
The computer is linked to a projector or interactive whiteboard	Yes/No
The chalkboard/penboard is in good condition	Yes/No

Any comments about the standard of equipment present, its use and/or any equipment that may be required in the room.

Your evaluation about this classroom
In your opinion, how welcoming is it, and what makes
it an interesting room to be in?

In your opinion, what additions or changes would this
classroom benefit from?

Other thoughts

Looking at the previous section, we can divide pupils'
needs into rapport, structure and creativity. Below is
a checklist of things *not* to be doing as far as rapport,
structure and creativity are concerned. Tick all the ones
you find yourself doing. Be honest!

Rapport

☐ Underestimating pupils' capabilities

Creative Teaching

- ☐ Communicating negative expectations
- ☐ Comparing pupils
- ☐ Having favourites
- ☐ Shouting a lot at your pupils
- ☐ Making pupils prove themselves
- ☐ Using ability as a way to measure self-worth
- ☐ Suggesting to pupils that ability is fixed
- ☐ Showing no interest in pupils
- ☐ You do not know pupils' names
- ☐ You do not know pupils' special educational needs
- ☐ You show active dislike or contempt for some pupils
- ☐ You show active dislike or contempt for a whole class (or classes)
- ☐ Not keeping promises
- ☐ Failing to admit your mistakes
- ☐ Not listening to your pupils
- ☐ Dismissing pupils' suggestions
- ☐ Using fear, motivation or intimidation

Structure

☐ You act as if you are superior

☐ You control for the sake of controlling, not for the sake of learning

☐ You do not explain to pupils what to do, you tell

☐ You impose oppressive rules that go beyond the school's rules

☐ You apply rules inconsistently

☐ You use empty threats/don't follow through on punishments you threaten

☐ You don't follow the rules

☐ You degrade or intimidate pupils

☐ You create uncertainty by not making clear expected outcomes

Creativity

☐ You set unattainable goals

☐ You create uncertainty through vague outcomes

☐ You show a lack of enthusiasm for what you are teaching

Creative Teaching

- [ ] You fail to explain the purpose and/or relevance of the material being covered

- [ ] There is little enjoyment of learning in your classroom

- [ ] Learning exercises overwhelmingly involve writing large amounts of text with pupils working by themselves

- [ ] There is a lack of pace

- [ ] Pupils seem bored in your lessons

- [ ] Pupils who misbehave claim that they are bored

- [ ] Your worksheets are mostly fill-in-the-gap exercises

- [ ] You do pupils' work for them

Ability to develop, or change, what you do presently

Think of when you last shouted at a class or at a pupil, did you choose to shout, or did you just lose your temper? Teaching is an act. No matter what kind of learning environment you have, pupils will misbehave. It is entirely natural that when you put 20 to 30 children together in one room they will not all get on with each other, with you or their work the entire time.

A creative classroom environment might do more to engage pupils who misbehave, but the reasons for their behaviour are complex and not entirely under your control by any means.

My point here is that there needs to be a level of professional detachment on your part that analyses how you conduct your own behaviour in your classroom. Have you smiled at the class? Did you remember to welcome them, tell them it was nice to see them again and then recap the previous lesson? What strategies do you have in place to deal with certain pupils in your class? What possibilities have you mentally prepared yourself for in terms of pupil behaviour? How will you deal with any attempts to sabotage your lesson (see fact box on sabotage below)? What funny things or interesting facts could you tell them? How does what they are learning today fit in with everything else they are doing, and what does it relate to that they might find familiar? What personal issues do you have, and can you make sure that these do not affect your attitude to your class?

If you have the ability to look at how you act in front of your pupils, and then amend your actions as necessary, you are more than halfway there. Teaching has to be something of an act, a performance, because otherwise you are just being too honest with your pupils. You leave yourself open to feeling upset and personally offended by pupils who are rude or don't work sufficiently well

Creative Teaching

for you. Because they are children, they are not fully in control of their feelings and emotions and will play up. Many badly behaved children at school grow up to regret the way they acted.

Unlike your pupils, you are in control of your feelings (think emotional intelligence) so why stress yourself out shouting away at your pupils or simply feeling depressed by their behaviour when you can act and react to them using your head instead? This means, for example, that if you shout, you've chosen to shout because you felt it was the most appropriate thing to do, not because you were getting angry. Such a judicial approach will most probably reduce the frequency with which you shout, and as such will make pupils take you far more seriously when, or preferably if, you do raise your voice.

Fact box 4: Sabotage

How do you handle attempts to sabotage your lesson? Pupils with behavioural issues will try to do things to draw attention to themselves, or apparently simply to annoy you! There are many reasons for this kind of behaviour which I don't need to discuss here, but you must not permit it because you leave yourself open to all sorts of problems and you are not doing your bit to ensure that such pupils become responsible citizens.

Nor can you simply tell them off or get angry with them; it may or may not deal with the current situation but it will do little to discourage future attempts at sabotaging your lessons. It is also not a very positive way to deal with it; you'll be reducing that pupil's dignity and can reduce your approachability in the eyes of that pupil and other pupils.

Remember that you cannot control pupils' behaviour, you can only influence it. So if a pupil misbehaves, it isn't likely to be your fault – it is the choice of the pupil to misbehave.

First you should remain calm within yourself. Will a joke or a (non-sarcastic) witticism alleviate the situation? If it is more serious, explain the situation to the pupil – preferably one-to-one rather than in front of the whole class – and explain why the pupil's behaviour is wrong, or why they need to do the given activity. Explaining why is always a good tactic (provided that there is a good reason 'why') as it allows you to justify why you are correct and the pupil is not correct without placing personal blame on the pupil. It is also wise to explain what the logical consequence will be if their current behaviour continues. It depersonalizes things somewhat, removing the suggestion that you dislike the pupil. It is just their behaviour you dislike.

You could also have something of a points system. It could be personalized, or it could relate to a schoolwide house points system for example. Personally, I like the idea of dividing the class up into teams – maybe ones relevant to the topic you are studying – and awarding points to that team for good work, good contribution to activities in class, and so on, while deducting points for bad behaviour or a lack of effort. A little bit of peer pressure should keep pupils behaving, especially if there is a good prize to be won. It doesn't have to be a money-based prize; it could be chocolate or (better still) the opportunity to do something such as perform in front of the class, or teach on a subject of their choice, for example.

Earlier I mentioned using the word 'and' instead of 'but' when giving pupils feedback. This is another example of using your head when teaching. By being aware of how you say things, you can do a lot to ensure a positive reaction from pupils, fostering a positive rapport and ultimately a more creative, secure learning environment.

Using accelerated learning

My company, Learning Performance, has been teaching accelerated learning techniques in schools since 1994. There are two parts to it: learning skills (or study skills) the pupils should use, and a model for learning that teachers should use with their pupils' active involvement.

Study Skills

Study Skills refer to a range of activities and techniques that pupils can use to make learning easier. To clarify, 'learning' in this instance means anything that has to be memorized and understood. So study skills are memory techniques, understanding and summarizing techniques and revision techniques. All three categories can be used in your creative teaching, but it will be the understanding techniques you will probably focus on most in class time.

Memory techniques come in two varieties. The variety that deals with memorizing those tricky little details and the variety that deals with memorizing whole topics of work or other major concepts. The most popular and familiar memory technique for little details is a mnemonic. This can, for instance, be where you take the first letter of each of the words to be recalled and use them to make up a silly sentence using the letters to start new words. So, for instance, in order to memorize both the names of the planets (Mercury, Venus, Earth, Mars, Jupiter, Saturn, Uranus, Neptune and Pluto) and the order they come in, you could say to yourself: *My Very Easy Method Just Speeds Up Naming Planets*, or more amusingly *My Very Energetic Mother Just Swam Under the North Pole*. The point of this technique is not to create another layer of things for the pupil to remember, but to create *triggers* that aid the pupil's learning. So the word 'planets' becomes associated with the silly mnemonic (which appeals to all sorts of imagination areas of the brain) and the first letters trigger the original words learnt.

Other similar techniques include peg words and image chains. A peg word is a word that rhymes with a number and can be easily visualized. You then get pupils to 'hook' each word to be memorized on a peg word. So, for instance, with a list of ten words you would get pupils to visualize the first thing on their list melting in the sun (because sun rhymes with one), or some other imaginative association they can make between the item and the peg word. Two's peg word could be shoe, three – tree, and so on. The reason for using a peg word is that numbers are not particularly tangible in the imagination, but a word easily associable with each is. You can have a lot of fun getting pupils to remember the list words at random, ask them for number seven on their list and I guarantee you it will trigger near-instant recall. Note that this is not about understanding, this is about remembering key words.

An image chain is a similar idea, but can be used quite a bit more flexibly than other memory techniques. Pupils need to use their imagination to visualize a series of images that depict the things they have to memorize. Think of it as being like a movie, a comic or a storyboard in their minds. Less tangible words that are hard to imagine can be substituted using the same first letter or a word that rhymes. Events in the story they will create will trigger the words they need to recall.

Study skills that are effective in dealing with whole topics or other coherent 'chunks' of information involve making sure that pupils understand the work fully too. By 'understanding' I am not only referring to whether or not a pupil 'gets it' but whether they can spot how information is interconnected, and how well they can break information down to its relevant component parts.

All information is organized. There is the overall theme, the main ideas – which act like chapter headings – and then the primary details which tend to give the who, what, why, when, where and how about the main ideas, and then the secondary (and tertiary, and so on) details which expand upon the primary details with examples, exceptions and the like. How many of your GCSE and A-level pupils could take a unit they have just been studying and break it down like this? The thing is, in order for them to be able to answer top-level exam questions sufficiently well this then is the skill that is required. If they understand the topic, they will be able to pick out the relevant parts to talk about and allude to all the right connected ideas.

The best way to combine both understanding and memorizing is to get pupils to map out topics or chunks. Maps are creative and logical diagrams that organize thoughts and help to formulate the structure of the information to be memorized. By using colour and images and by forcing the mind to be logical, mapping combines both right and left brain very effectively and engages most people's RAS. There are some guidelines to getting this technique right. First, maps are not brainstorms or spider diagrams; words and images should be written or drawn directly onto the lines, not in bubbles floating off somewhere else. This helps the mind associate and recall things in the right place. Second, less is more. Keywords, not sentences, should go on the map; neither is this the place for masses of detail, triggers should be used instead. Here's an outline of what a good map could look like:

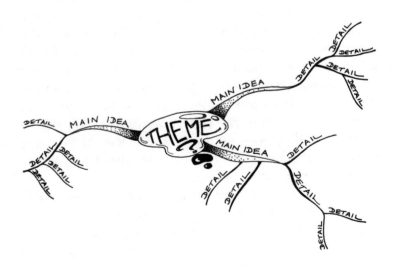

It is not restricted to just two or three main branches, but I would not recommend more than six because then it becomes rather cluttered. The final guideline is that the reason this technique works is because the pupils have been actively involved in making the map, quite independent of you the teacher. So do not make maps for your pupils, let them make the maps themselves. You might, of course, like to point them in the right direction with things to include on the map!

The last study skill to look at is revision. It always amazes us at Learning Performance how few pupils know how to do this properly, and how few schools do a lot to help them with this. It is ironic that the one aspect of the learning process that pupils have complete control over is the one they find most boring. But the boredom is somewhat unnecessary, as are the numerous tortuous hours spent revising – or rather cramming – in the run-up to the exams. Pupils, and teachers, often get revision and relearning mixed up. If pupils look at their notes, do not recall what the information is about and then start breaking the information down into its component parts, that is not revision. Revision is when pupils look at their notes, recognize the information and can recall it, test themselves and compare it with their original notes, spot their successes and identify areas to be relearned or reinforced. Surely the word 'revision' means to 'look again'? Not to 'learn again'.

Creative Teaching

Creative teachers can help pupils revise by giving them first summary exercises to do for homework, such as a mapping exercise, and then doing recall tests in class. These tests do not have to be strict exam-style tests (although there is a place for doing so); it could simply be redrawing maps, or playing games such as Trivial Pursuit but with questions on your subject – the pupils could have prepared the questions themselves, or you can often purchase memory flashcards which should be suitable.

Knowledge of how to teach creatively: the philosophy of the creative classroom

The creative classroom enhances learning in two ways: it makes learning more enjoyable, and it enables pupils to produce better work. The philosophy of the creative classroom is that *learning is most effective when it is fun* (Peter Kline, *The Everyday Genius**). By *fun* I do not mean that you need to be funnier than Lee Evans and more inventive than Johnny Ball. And there are topics that are simply not meant to be 'fun', in fact they are very serious. By *fun* Peter Kline really means that you are not going to learn very effectively if you are bored.

* Kline, P. (1997) *The Everyday Genius: Restoring Children's Natural Joy of Learning, and Yours Too.* Salt Lake City, UT: Great River Books.

How can you take what you do at the moment and make it better? For instance, I recently had to teach my GCSE Religious Studies class about the how the Sunni/Shia split came about in Islam. To be honest with you, it wasn't going to be a particularly good lesson. The split occurred simply because some of the followers of Muhammad couldn't agree on who should be their new leader. Pupils have to learn the names of the main players and how they relate to each other. We were reading from the textbook, and pupils were simply going to write answers to the questions in the book. Nothing wrong with that, but they were not going to be particularly interested in the exercise (they are a very kinaesthetic group) and, as such, they would probably not remember the topic so easily – or at best resent having to revise, or relearn, it later on.

As we were reading through the text, one pupil said, 'I'm getting really confused!' and others chimed in agreement. No big surprise. So I suggested that we make a diagram on the board. It's a class of 16 pupils, it wasn't hard to gather them around and get them to take it in turns to write up the next name on the board and doodle important information next to names, and so on. The pupils understood it all much better when they had participated in discovering the information for themselves (well, OK, with a little help from me) and mapped it out as a team. Moreover, they enjoyed themselves. Then they copied it down, answering many of the questions in the textbook, but in a diagram instead.

It's not much of a stretch of an idea to get the pupils to make the diagram physically, with each pupil (or a group of pupils) representing a key person or piece of information in this story. It would make for a good review exercise.

If pupils are engaged, interested and enjoying themselves, then it is important to make sure the structure is there for them to improve their learning performance. There needs to be an improvement in standards of work and grades to make this all worthwhile. And, of course, when I set a piece of written work about the split, my pupils wrote excellent work that showed a clear understanding of what took place and the ramifications it had for Islam. They applied what they had learned to the questions asked without any real direct input from me and they succeeded. Even those who were struggling in my subject and elsewhere performed well in this assignment. It goes to show that once motivated, and when taking responsibility for their own learning, there is a lot a pupil can achieve.

Creativity with a healthy dose of independent learning is the key to making learning more effective.

So step 1 to achieve our philosophy is to ensure that the pupils feel secure with you and in your environment. This will allow and enable creativity. Step 2 is to make sure all your pupils feel valued. This will encourage confidence and positive participation in your lessons. You don't want a two-tier classroom set-up, where some pupils become stars at this kind of thing and the others become passive observers. Step 3 is to encourage feelings of personal responsibility for their work and to empower pupils to be more autonomous so that their learning performance, including their ability to learn for themselves, improves.

Here's a breakdown of those three steps, and some self-evaluation opportunities for you to consider where you are at in each step and what you might like to do to develop each step.

Step 1: Security

Pupils need to have the freedom to be themselves, and the coherent structure to prevent utter anarchy. This is the most fundamental thing to cater for when establishing a creative classroom.

Creativity is an expression of the self, so if pupils cannot be themselves in your classroom, then their creativity will be inhibited for fear of judgement from you or from their peers. However, there needs to be a clear framework for learning in your classroom too. Freedom to be themselves does not equate with freedom not to work or freedom to annoy other pupils and their teacher!

Creative Teaching

Pupils need to come into your classroom knowing that they will be safe – that they are highly unlikely to be made a fool of (by their peers or their teacher), to worry, to feel stupid, to feel unappreciated or unwanted and to leave unrewarded for their effort. Instead they will come to expect your classroom to be a place where they feel welcomed, their opinions are valued, they learn and develop, and they know what the rules are, understand them and are willing to follow them.

Using our three headings from earlier – rapport, structure and creativity – use the checklist below to consider what you do already to encourage a sense of security among pupils in your classroom. Then pick something from each list that you could try out in your classroom.

Rapport

☐ You communicate positive expectations

☐ You show that you want to get to know pupils

☐ You can greet pupils by name

☐ You express tasks as learning processes, not evaluations

☐ You emphasize the importance of putting in effort, rather than the importance of ability

- [ ] You actively demonstrate an interest in and enjoyment of teaching

- [ ] You actively demonstrate an enjoyment of your subject

- [ ] You realize when a pupil is not feeling well

Structure

- [ ] You set limits without being oppressive or over-controlling

- [ ] You emphasize the goals and the purpose of learning

- [ ] You communicate and explain rules and routines clearly

- [ ] You apply rules, routines and penalties consistently

- [ ] You apply penalties because of the pupil's behaviour, not because of the pupil's character

- [ ] You express rules in terms of appropriate, rather than prohibited, behaviour

- [ ] You have authority and can exercise control

- [ ] You make clear expected outcomes

- [ ] Pupils will know what to expect in your lessons when it comes to behaviour and routine

Creative Teaching

Creativity

- [ ] You show enthusiasm for your subject
- [ ] You explain why
- [ ] You set appropriate, attainable goals
- [ ] You highlight the importance/usefulness of the work
- [ ] You give clear instructions and objectives
- [ ] You increase pupils' knowledge and understanding
- [ ] You try to make lessons enjoyable and stimulating
- [ ] You use differentiated materials when appropriate
- [ ] You take the lead; you are the expert, informing learners
- [ ] You use a range of learning activities

Step 2: Being valued

In addition to enabling pupils to be themselves, the next thing you need to foster in your pupils is a sense of intrinsic worth. Children and teenagers can be emotionally insecure, so while you might be able to look after issues of external security, you need to draw out pupils' creative nature. In younger children, creativity is often not a difficulty, but teenagers often doubt their own abilities in this area (as well as in others). If you appear to value pupils' input, praise their positive contributions to your lessons, and combine this with the secure environment you create in your classroom, then pupils will be more motivated and respond more enthusiastically and effectively to your lessons.

As with the previous checklist, tick the things you already do to make pupils feel valued and pick one thing from each list that you could try to do.

Rapport

☐ You know your pupils' characters

☐ You create a non-judgemental environment in your classroom

☐ You emphasize, and appreciate, what each pupil is good at

☐ You encourage pupils to develop their interests rather than please you

☐ You encourage pupils to improve themselves rather than prove themselves

☐ You believe, and make clear this belief to your

pupils, that if you believe you can, or believe you can't, then you're right

☐ You focus on individual progress and achievement, rather than comparison

☐ You encourage pupils to ask questions and express their opinions

☐ You always remind pupils how much they are learning

☐ You show your pupils the many ways to be successful

☐ You admit, and apologize, if you are wrong

☐ You ask your pupils for feedback about their experience of learning in your lessons

Structure

☐ Although you make pupils accountable, you try not to use your authority in an imposing manner

☐ You help pupils to set realistic goals for themselves

☐ You encourage pupils to use sensible self-control, rather than giving them lots of petty instructions

☐ You recognize that pupils have feelings

☐ You don't take yourself too seriously and exercise a sense of humour

☐ Your pupils willingly agree to rules and learning objectives

Creativity

☐ You try to create curiosity through variety

☐ You encourage pupils to use their creative side

☐ You adapt teaching methods to pupils' learning styles

☐ You allow pupils to perform to the limits of their ability, and you set them challenges to push their ability further

☐ You engage pupils through activities like problem-solving, role-play and simulation

☐ Pupils have a sense that the work being completed is relevant and meaningful

☐ You relate the curriculum to pupils' own lives and experiences

☐ You utilize what pupils are interested in and think is relevant in your lessons

☐ You emphasize the learning process

Creative Teaching

☐ You use kinaesthetic activities in your lessons

☐ You expect positivity and participation from pupils

Stage 3: Independent learning

One of the biggest changes that took place in the twentieth century was the nature of the workplace. So many companies today expect their employees to be able to learn new skills whenever necessary. It could be argued that the outcomes of schooling are now more focused on transferable skills than on academic knowledge, reflecting the relentless march of the information age: what you were able to do yesterday may be out of date by tomorrow.

Moreover, if pupils feel they have an element of control and input into their learning, then they will participate far more effectively in the process of learning. By control I don't mean that they dictate the agenda – you know best, as teacher you are still the expert; instead I mean their ability to evaluate their own progress, to spot for themselves the skills they can learn from an activity, and to be entrusted not to go off-task when asked to discuss something with their neighbour. This is obviously something which requires a degree of maturity, and full autonomy would be something I would expect from A-level pupils, but for it to work without great upheaval at that age, it can be encouraged in younger pupils, from around the age of ten in Years 6 and 7 (P7 and S1 in Scotland).

As before, tick the things you currently find yourself doing and highlight something from each list you think you might like to try.

Rapport

☐ You encourage students to give positive feedback to each other

☐ You ask your pupils about what helps them to learn best, and respond appropriately

☐ You accept feedback from pupils neutrally and calmly

☐ Pupils in your class are confident that you know them and understand them well

Structure

☐ The focus is on learning, not on you

☐ You encourage pupil autonomy by giving pupils

leadership roles, choices, a share of responsibilities and opportunities for decision-making

☐ You help pupils to develop skills that enable them to take responsibility for their learning and solve their own problems

☐ You allow pupils to set their own schedules, choose their own work methods, what order they will work on tasks, take breaks, etc.

Creativity

☐ You enable pupils to learn things for themselves: there is a feeling of discovery in your lessons

☐ You help pupils set realistic goals for themselves

☐ You model the attitudes you expect from pupils, such as patience, persistence and learning from mistakes

☐ You help pupils to create their own ways of learning something

☐ You encourage pupils to reorganize and review their notes

These checklists contain a series of ideas and attitudes that you can employ in your teaching to facilitate the development of your creative classroom environment. Getting creative teaching right is far more about what you think and how you act upon those thoughts, rather than simply employing a range of fancy teaching tricks.

If you just start introducing creative learning activities without much regard for the context in which they should be conducted, then you run the risk of everything falling flat. Without the right rapport in place, pupils won't appreciate the effort you've gone to, or the purpose of the activity. If pupils don't feel safe and valued with you, then they may be reluctant to participate effectively, or underestimate their ability to do the activity. Without a good discipline structure in place, pupils may sabotage your activity, and use the unusual level of autonomy you've granted them to disrupt others' learning, bully and/or undermine your authority and confidence.

Hopefully you've identified a lot of things that you already do to foster creativity, and can identify some other things you could try to do. With these in place, you should feel free to experiment with some of the ideas to get you started on the next page. I've divided them up into the steps identified above. You should feel free and confident to come up with your own ideas – my ideas are just a trigger to get you thinking.

The learning process in the creative classroom

There is a line of educational theory that says lessons should start with a statement of objectives followed by a starter activity, then the main learning activities and finally a plenary to reinforce the learning. A similar process applies to a unit of work too. You introduce the topic with an overview, followed by lessons that study aspects of the topic and always point back to the overview, and you finish the topic by making sure that all the pupils see how the lessons all fit together using the overview. Both make perfect sense. But there is a problem, and the problem is reality.

In my last school, lessons were 40 minutes long. It was not really possible to have starter activities, because with the best will in the world any meaningful activity will take up more than five minutes. And, besides, how is any teacher actually meant to invent that number of exciting starter activities? In my opinion, starter activities are good at the start of a new unit, or they are good to 'warm up' an unmotivated or tired class, and as such do not need to come at the start of a lesson.

Creative teaching must follow a clear structure in order to make sure that meaningful learning takes place; but that structure should not be too rigid as otherwise it will cause you too many difficulties. Start lessons with a recap of previous relevant learning so that pupils understand where this lesson will fit in.

A question-and-answer session is fine, but there are some more inventive ideas below. Then state the lesson objective by telling the pupils simply what they will be able to do by the end of the lesson. Stating lesson objectives is an important thing to do because, to alter the famous saying, if pupils don't know where you are taking them, they won't realize when they get there.

Make sure you state the objectives in some active form. Simply stating 'By the end of the lesson you will know about the cause of the Second World War' is not good enough because it allows pupils to become passive as they wait for the knowledge somehow to become known to them. It would be better to say 'By the end of the lesson you will have discovered the causes of the Second World War' and maybe to add icing to the cake: 'and you will be able to reflect upon and analyse the repercussions that events can have in history'.

Ideas to get you started: lesson starters, recall activities and warm-ups

Things to remember

Imagine that you are about to start a lesson. When your pupils arrive in your classroom, you must, must,

must remember that your pupils have a life outside of your classroom. This means that there is a period of time from the end of your last lesson and the start of this one where pupils have experienced many other things. You certainly have, because contrary to popular pupil opinion, you don't live in your classroom. In fact, if you thought hard enough, you could probably list a hundred things you did since you saw your pupils last. And you have not been on the receiving end of lesson after lesson, homework after homework. So you need to bring pupils' minds to where they were in your last lesson: you need to revise what has been learned already.

Also, given that you haven't been responsible for their emotional welfare in that intervening time, you don't know what mood your pupils are going to be in. The teacher of their last lesson could have been your school's version of Grotbags, and they could all be really riled up and tense. Or they could be hyper because of the soft touch Joyce Grenfell-esque teacher who doesn't really have any classroom control. Or worse, some were with Grotbags while the others were with Joyce Grenfell, meaning you have a mixture of both tense and hyper.

Moreover, what about everything else going on? What about how well they are getting on with their friends? What about problems at home? What pressures and issues are affecting them? In many instances you just don't know; a lot may have happened since last lesson and as such pupils' behaviour, mood, attention and interest could be very different from the last time you saw them. It's worth remembering that your lesson is very unlikely to be the most important thing in their lives. You need to get their attention. A strict teacher will often do this with a shout and a bit of fear motivation. However, following the philosophy of the creative classroom means you need to enter them into the spirit and mindset of your lesson in a more positive fashion. So your lesson starters should be something of a motivational warm-up as well as a bit of revision.

Smile. Whatever mood you are really in, it doesn't matter, it is important to make sure you are in your creative state, so from the moment you see a pupil, smile! Act as though nothing is a problem for you and you are pleased to see them. It will make all the difference.

Remember to say hello ('Good morning, class') – it's only polite – and say something nice about them ('It's good to see you again') to make them feel valued.

Also remember that a pupil has only learned what they have memorized. If they don't remember it, they haven't learned it. If during your lesson starter you realize that the class in general has forgotten something, then look for ways to reintroduce the forgotten concept/ information to reinforce it.

Creative Teaching

Some Ideas

A moment's thought

Having said hello, tell your pupils that you're going to give them a moment (thirty seconds to one minute, up to you) to recall everything they learned last lesson. They should jot down as many points as they can on a piece of paper or the back of their exercise books.

♦ You might like to give them a minimum number of points to write down; three might be a good starting place.

♦ Make it into something of a game, pile on mock pressure as time runs out, give lots of motivational praise and/or encourage a little friendly rivalry with their neighbour to see how many points each has written down.

♦ If a pupil genuinely cannot remember anything from last lesson, then use a series of prompts with them as everyone else gets on with the activity. Ask them if they can remember the gist, or the topic. It may well be the case that they can remember some of it, but find it hard to write it down. This is OK. You might like to try the next idea instead if this is the case with many of your pupils.

♦ You could reward the person/people who got the most number of points, for example a credit for your school's merit system.

Without asking for hands up (it allows pupils to opt out too easily, particularly in this scenario), ask random pupils for one thing they wrote down on their list and, if the point is correct and relevant, ask the class how many got that on their list. Asking random pupils means that pupils make sure they are ready to answer and are therefore better engaged. Involving the whole class means that everyone gets involved and the pupil receives peer acknowledgement for getting it right.

♦ If the pupil is wrong, don't scold. Throw it open to the class to correct the misunderstanding, but do so in a friendly manner. For example, 'Thank you, but that's not everything we need to know, can anyone tell us what's missing?'

Make sure you then make the link between what they've remembered and what they are about to learn in your lesson. Tell them what they are going to be able to do or what they will know about by the end of the lesson.

Creative additions to this idea

At the end of the starter, assuming that pupils wrote down their ideas on a piece of paper, get them to fold up the paper into paper aeroplanes. Place the waste bin in the middle of the room and get pupils to aim for the bin. There's no particular reason for this activity, other than to dispose of scrap paper in a reasonably kinaesthetic way. It will help your kinaesthetic pupils get involved in your lesson if they've had a chance to make something and move about a bit.

If you are doing this with excitable pupils for the first time, explain to them that attempts to sabotage this game will result in points being deducted from your points system, or some other simple equivalent.

Think pair share

Follow the same steps as with *A moment's thought* but instead of a class discussion, get pupils to talk to their neighbour. Give pupils up to a minute to 'think' and then give pupils another minute to 'pair and share' what they've recalled with their neighbour. It's a less exposing way of achieving the same kind of revision as *A moment's thought*. Working in a pair will probably correct many mistakes, although if you're not sure, you can always still have the class feedback element too.

Bob if you ...

Bobbing is the art of raising yourself out of your seat a little bit, and then sitting back down. The effect is that you 'bob up' from your seat. It's the kinaesthetic equivalent of putting your hand up. Pupils find this a far more fun and interactive way of participating.

Simply question the class and get them to respond in the positive by bobbing up. So, for instance, you could say in History 'The Second World War began in 1939' and check for pupils' knowledge by seeing how many bobbed up in agreement. You could mix it in with false statements to see if you could catch anyone out. Alternatively you could use multiple-answer questions and get pupils to bob up for answer a, b, c or d.

Interactive fun

If you're lucky enough to have a projector or interactive whiteboard in your classroom, then you might like to use it to play warm-up games. For example, you could combine *Bob if you . . .* with *Who Wants to be a Millionaire?* which you can download from www.csfsoftware.co.uk. It's fully customizable, so you can enter your own questions and answer options. Moreover it's free! You can also download other interactive games like their *Countdown* emulator.

What am I?

Instead of asking a question, give them the answer and get them to work out what the question is. In Maths, you could give the answer '20' and pupils would have to think of all the ways to get to 20, 10×2, 5×4, $50 - 30$, and so on. In Geography you could start describing the features of something like an archipelago, and a pupil would have to guess what you are talking about.

Map it
When starting a new unit of work, get pupils to create the start of a map. Put the unit title in the centre, and the main ideas on branches. It's important that they make their own mind-maps so that they have a feeling of ownership over their work. Then at the start of the lesson, pupils add on details they have learned. For more information about how to map, see pp. 83–5.

Ideas to get you started: lesson middlers

Things to remember

OK, so 'middlers' is not a word. But I'm sure you understand what I mean. Middlers are the main activities of your lesson. By necessity they may well involve large amounts of written work – for instance, GCSE coursework or an essay – but remember that pupils do not learn only if they can present you with neatly written answers to textbook questions. Remember that they are more likely to learn better, and recall the information, through more active methods and can then produce superior written work as a summative exercise.

One of the things you will notice is that the activities often involve providing pupils with the core information and getting them to be creative with it. Remember, this is the point of creative teaching – yes, you need to feel and be creative, come up with ideas and engage them through your personality and through your chosen activities, but, moreover, you want to facilitate an active creative approach among your pupils. So it is important not to spoon-feed them, you are aiming to give them independence and responsibility.

Some ideas

The learning factor
This is a really simple and very flexible idea where pupils can work individually, in pairs or in groups. Simply give out the information you want pupils to learn, it could be pages from a textbook, newspaper articles, a video or something else. Give them a time limit, maybe 20 minutes, to come up with a song or a rap to perform to the rest of the class about the given topic. You can stipulate certain things they must include, but I am sure you'll be impressed with just how much they include themselves.

Drawing blind
If you have an image of something pupils need to be

familiar with, such as a place of worship, a geographical feature or location, parts of an experiment, or maybe the mechanism of an object, then get pupils to copy it down from the OHP or digital projector. However, the pupil drawing it should have their back to the image and should be relying on their partner to describe the image for them, attempting to communicate well enough to get a close replica of the image! It is great fun, and excellent for all sorts of communication and inter-personal skills. Pupils should then label the image with relevant information and amend any serious errors!

Conversion
Pupils simply need to convert the given information into some other form. It could be into 'txt spk', or into a flow diagram, a map, a table, a picture, or even a play!

On the move
Pair up pupils and give them a question or issue to discuss for two minutes. They should spend time listening to each other's opinions and, for higher ability or older pupils, they should then see where they have similarities and differences of opinions. Everyone then gets up and swaps partners. This can be done in a variety of ways. You could be very orderly and have arranged pupils to sit in two circles – an inner and an outer circle – facing each other. This has the advantage of being able quickly to move pupils in one circle round a bit so they find

new partners. The disadvantage is that you will need to have moved the furniture in your room, which is part of creative teaching. However, in the event of furniture moving not being possible, then you could arrange new pairings in different ways. You could tell pupils to find a new partner who 'is sitting furthest from you', 'is a member of the same sex', or the other sex, 'has the same coloured hair', 'whose name shares a letter with a letter with yours', and so on. The new partnership has to explain their previous partner's point of view and then take the discussion on further. It's great for listening skills, which should wake your pupils up! Plus it is an inventive way to spice up discussions.

Advertising

You always remember the things you see in adverts, so why not use adverts as a teaching tool? This activity takes two forms. Again, provide pupils with the information, but this time get them to prepare a billboard advertisement as if the information were a film or a product to be sold. Alternatively, get your pupils to write and perform a movie trailer of the information. I really enjoyed my Year 12's movie trailer for 'Aristotle: the greatest philosopher that walked this Earth'!

The little things

Sometimes it is the simplest ideas that work the best. If you can use chocolates or sweets, then you are on to a winner. Demonstrate the causes of erosion by getting the class to put a sweet in their mouths. Demonstrate the necessary existence of God by using chocolate – which is better, chocolate that you imagine or chocolate that is real? You can be healthy and use fruit if you prefer. Anything that helps pupils visualize what you are talking about is helpful. You could demonstrate the effects of rationing by putting on your table a day's worth of food allowance, but it would be far simpler to pour out some jelly beans on a desk, tell them the beans represent how much they get to eat daily today and then separate off roughly the right proportion to represent how much they would have got after the Second World War.

Ideas to get you started: lesson enders

Things to remember

It is important to end the lesson neatly and clearly. It is best if you can recap what has been learned in the lesson by testing them quickly. As 80 per cent of detail can be forgotten within 24 hours of learning it, it makes a big difference if you reinforce it before they go. While pupils will inevitably forget information and details you teach them if they do not reinforce it in their own time (the neural pathways will degrade over time if they are not lit up often enough), if you reinforce the learning before you dismiss your class then that 80 per cent becomes more like 40 per cent or 50 per cent, which is not great, but is better. If you also recap and test their memories at the start of your next lesson with them, then again you significantly reduce the amount they will forget because you are lighting up the right neural pathways.

Some ideas

Quickfire list
Get pupils to jot down five things they have learned in your lesson. If there's time, get them to explain one or two of these things to a neighbour.

On trial
Get the pupils to vote, as if they were a jury, on the most important thing or things learned in your lesson. This does a great job of highlighting the main ideas.

Mission completed?
State the lesson objective again – can your pupils fulfil the objective? Ask random pupils (do not accept hands-up as it allows other pupils to become passive).

Creative Teaching

Newsflash
Pupils simply prepare a quick news report on your lesson. Get them to perform it if there's time – you can always pair up the groups so that they can perform to each other instead of the whole class. Better still, get them to perform it at the start of next lesson as a recap activity.

Tableau
Get pupils to form a tableau – a sort of 'freeze-frame moment' – of something learned in the lesson (for example, a scene in a book they are reading, or a nature cycle represented in human form) and then quiz individuals in the tableau about the 'character' they are playing.

End as you began
Most of the lesson starters also make good plenary activities too, so don't forget them! Remember that any approach you use at any time can be used at most points in the learning process. So have fun and enjoy seeing just what creative things your pupils are capable of!

3 The creative school

Schools that are getting it right

Our team of presenters at Learning Performance have, between them, conducted over 8,000 workshops in schools, meeting well over 1 million pupils. These are some of their best memories of schools and teaching staff that have engaged pupils successfully in the creative learning process ...

There was this one school I visited which had a really different feel to it. There was a kind of buzz in the air and it was a very cheerful, friendly place. But that isn't what made it different. Plenty of schools are like that. What was noticeable was that age wasn't much of a barrier. In fact pupils walked around in mixed age groups. You see, they had what the school called 'vertical forms' – instead of grouping their form classes by year group they organized

Creative Teaching

them in house teams where Year 7 through to Year 11 pupils were together in the same form class. The school swears by this system. They told me it created scope for mentoring younger pupils, and indeed it encouraged greater maturity among their younger pupils as they were in direct contact with their older peers. It goes to show you what a little out-of-the-box thinking can do.

I've been visiting the same school each year for the last six years. When I first arrived the teachers were understandably sceptical about what I was teaching their pupils, but by the end of the day they were onboard and seemed really enthused by the ideas we were talking about. The next time I went back, one of the teachers greeted me with a big smile and took me to her classroom to show me what she had been up to since the last time I was there. She had got her pupils mapping out their work, and there must have been a hundred association maps around the room, all produced by her pupils. She told me that they used to do brainstorms, but since I demonstrated how to map things out she'd gone map crazy. She told me that pupils loved doing them as they were colourful and almost therapeutic to do, but they were great for summarizing and reinforcing all the information they had been learning. She says she gets less of a 'brain drain' when she tests pupils or revisits topics that they have mapped out. I find that the more creative schools are the ones where teachers are keen to show me what they do in their classrooms, like this lady was.

The creative school

I was doing an INSET day in a school, talking about the need to appeal to pupils' left and right brains. One of the maths teachers came up to me during the break and told me about his absolutely brilliant idea: darts. He got his pupils to play darts (I assume the Velcro variety, but you never know, it might be the real thing). They played darts and had to add up the score as quickly as possible and subtract it from the overall score. The pupils got competitive – in a good way – as they all tried to call out the correct score before anyone else did. They all had fun, and they were all doing mental arithmetic. Who'd have thought it possible?!

One very telling thing about schools is how willing staff are to join in with our activities. If they just sit in the corner marking work or, worse still, reading the paper, then you know that this is a school that is missing a trick. I know that staff have pressures to get work done, and marking is very important, but sometimes you can just tell that that member of staff is just disillusioned with their job. In schools that are more enjoyable places for both staff and pupils you'll find that the teachers will join in. They might just help pupils with the activities as we do them. Or they might be willing to come up to the front with me and demonstrate something. I have a very fond memory of a headteacher who helped me teach the pupils the kinaesthetic way to learn Japanese numbers, you know 'Itchy, knee, sun . . .'. He knew it and had a whale of a time getting the pupils to do it. They responded well and clearly

Creative Teaching

liked him. It makes so much of a difference if this kind of creative input comes from the top.

One school I visited had focused on languages and, as a way to engage pupils, one of the language teachers had translated scripts of TV shows and got the pupils to perform them. Pupils didn't necessarily know all the language, but they learned it pretty quickly because they all recognized the episode and so were able to directly relate to what was being said. In lots of schools I go to, pupils rate language subjects as some of their least favourite usually because they don't see it as relevant. But not at this school, the kids loved it.

Manners make a big difference. In some schools, and it can be anywhere in the country, pupils don't have manners. They don't seem to respect the school or the people in it and, as a result, don't seem to care very much about learning. But in schools where the pupils are nice to you and to each other they are more ready to learn. I went to one school and just as I got out of my car a pupil asked me if I wanted a sweet and I just knew I was going to have a good day! This was reflected across the whole school as far as I could see. There was no animosity in my group, everyone was friendly, everyone seemed to enjoy themselves and had a great time learning. You couldn't achieve that sort of situation in a school where pupils didn't have manners. A friendly environment is essential I think.

Building the creative school

So you've read about creating a more motivating, creative classroom environment, and you've decided upon a few things you would like to try out. But what about what goes on outside of your classroom? Most pupils will spend more than one-quarter of their time in school outside of lessons. And I'm not talking about pupils who bunk off. Form/registration time, assemblies, break and lunch times all add up to a considerable amount of time spent out of the classroom.

So what does your school do with its pupils to foster creativity, encourage a good attitude to learning and stimulate their RAS during out-of-classroom time? You might like to write in your thoughts to the questions about form/registration time and assemblies below, we'll come to break and lunch times later.

Form/registration time

What activities have you and your colleagues used in this time to foster creativity and engage pupils effectively, preparing them for learning?

What activities and policies do your senior management encourage or require you to do in this time, beyond taking the register and reading the notices?

119

Creative Teaching

Assemblies

Tick any of the following that apply.

☐ I don't go to assemblies as they are boring and I can get on with marking instead.

☐ I don't mind going to assemblies.

☐ I don't mind going to assemblies, and sometimes I'll even learn something I didn't know!

☐ Assemblies do a lot to motivate pupils for the day, with a good strong focus on things that are relevant to the pupils.

☐ A range of staff get involved in running assemblies.

☐ Pupils seem to enjoy assemblies.

☐ Pupils do not seem to like assemblies.

☐ Pupils are passive during assemblies, and in their opinion of assemblies.

☐ There is scope for doing more to improve the content of assemblies.

☐ There is scope for doing more to improve the conduct of assemblies.

Your responses should be something of an indication of how creative your school is. If teachers and management are bothered enough to attempt to create stimulating assemblies and enjoyable form times, then this will have an impact on the pupils' attitude to the school. Pupils will notice that people are trying to make their time as well spent as possible, and will (eventually) be appreciative. Moreover, they will be better prepared mentally for learning; they will be more positive and more receptive in class. And these are the principal reasons for encouraging the creative school ethos: it helps pupils to enjoy learning and improves their learning performance. It is not solely up to teachers in their classrooms to encourage and enable pupils; if such pockets of creativity are to be prevented then there needs to be a team effort from staff at all levels.

What I suggest you do is to link up with some other like-minded staff to look at implementing some of the ideas below. Maybe there are already means to coordinate such things in your school, in which case you should speak to people on the relevant committees to find out what ideas they have got in the pipeline. Maybe there are not the means, and you should discuss with members of your senior management team any ideas you have for improving creativity across the school.

The basis for creativity across the school is the same as in your classroom. Pupils need to know how to learn, and suitable attempts need to be made to engage with their RAS and their multiple intelligences to stimulate a positive attitude towards learning. Their emotional intelligence will be developed; and they will feel safe, welcomed and valued.

There are two parts to a successful whole-school approach to developing creativity: education and example. Education in the creative skills mentioned above is the initial reaction of many schools. They get a study skills company in for the day, the pupils learn about how to learn and have a great time. In fact at least one-third of UK secondary schools do this, as that is how many my company visited in 2004/5. Of course, the impact of visiting experts presenting to your pupils, and your staff, cannot be underestimated. Anything that stands out will engage with people's RAS, and collapsing the curriculum for the day and having in fun and entertaining people will certainly do that. Any good study skills day will have taught the pupils a range of skills, and most importantly that learning is not something that happens to them, it is something they make happen. But such an event is most effective when it is part of a school's wider effort to enhance pupils' learning performance and learning experience.

So the next step is a series of lessons on *learning to learn* in PSHE, or some other similar subject. Again, this is good because it gives pupils the ability to put more strategies to the test and find out more about how they learn. Self-reflection can be encouraged and a more mature approach to learning can be developed. They will know from their study skills day that learning is something they must involve themselves in, and from a good *learning to learn* course they will get a far better opportunity to work out how to get involved.

However, this is not much use if it is something studied in isolation. The rest of their school experience must live up to the strategies and ideals taught. It is no use to pupils if you tell them that they should summarize their units and make maps of them if teachers give them no opportunity to make maps. Pupils are not going to have much luck fostering their own creativity if they do not get opportunities to be creative in their classes. In fact, the best *learning to learn* courses in school are not limited to PSHE, nor are they limited to pupils. Teachers must know and accept these creative learning techniques. They are nothing new, they are not fads; they are tried and tested ideas that are founded on strong educational theory. Now, while you cannot realistically convince all teachers of the merits of creativity as outlined in this book, many teachers today are on the side of the ethos of these teaching and learning ideas and would appreciate a coordinated whole-school approach.

The first step would be to have an INSET on learning, training them in the kind of information in this book if necessary, and discussing the approaches your school will adopt. You could get teachers to create displays around the school on the different learning styles, or with motivational quotes about learning. Better still, you could get departments to review a scheme of work to see how to improve it by incorporating some creative learning into it. Such a day should be both motivational and full of strong educational substance and opportunity – not fluff or so many items that no quality time is spent on any one thing.

As well as this, the *learning to learn* lessons should extend across the curriculum. For instance, if multiple intelligences were examined in the relevant subjects, pupils would gain an idea of their strengths and weaknesses in each area. It would also help teachers to appreciate each pupil's learning needs more effectively.

Most importantly, the same teachers should work with the same pupils as often as possible. This allows a decent and effective relationship to be formed where a pupil has a much better chance of receiving a personalized and relevant education as the teacher properly understands the best way to teach each of his or her pupils. I appreciate the downsides from both the administration point of view and the situation where a teacher might be tormented by a relentless bully of a pupil, but in such a situation the good creative school will have effective measures in place to deal with this child's particular issues. 'Time Out' zones, counselling and one-to-one tutoring by a senior member of staff are all examples of an effective approach.

I would also suggest that a creative school form a learning profile for each pupil. Perhaps a sheet of A4

would be sufficient, summarizing any learning difficulties the child has, plus results from a VAK test,
findings from MI tests, observations from their form
tutor and other key staff about what the pupil is
good at doing (negatives would be unnecessary), plus
comments from the pupil themselves about what they
like doing at school, what their goals are, and so on.
Whenever a teacher taught a class, or a pupil, for the
first time, they would see this profile which outlined all
the good and useful things about a pupil.

The creative school should lead not only by education
but also by example, and a learning profile is one way in
which a school could lead by example. It is all very well
talking the talk with *learning to learn* courses and INSETs,
but it is largely in vain if you do not also walk the walk.
If the school does not 'feel' creative, or – worse still – is
oppressive in the way it operates, then pupils will not feel
empowered to follow suit and develop their creativity.

Maslow's Hierarchy of Needs is a well-known tool,
and I suggest you use it to analyse how well your school
meets pupils' needs and creates the right environment
for learning.

Abraham Maslow was born in 1908 in New York. As
his parents were uneducated Jewish immigrants, they
pushed their son towards academic success. Because of
this, as a child, he was quite isolated, spending most of
his time with books. He went on to study psychology
and gained his PhD in 1934. It is fair to say that his goal

was to make psychology relevant, more human than a whole load of theorizing.

Early in his career Maslow worked with monkeys. It interested him that some needs took precedence over others. For example, if you are hungry and thirsty you tend to quench your thirst first because you can go without food for longer than you can without water. Likewise, if you are extremely thirsty but someone has got you in a headlock and you cannot breathe, which is more important? The need to breathe, of course. So Maslow took this idea and created his well-known hierarchy of needs. Although they are not scientifically tested, they seem to have rung true with most people and there seems to be little for people to disagree with. Here is a diagram of the hierarchy:

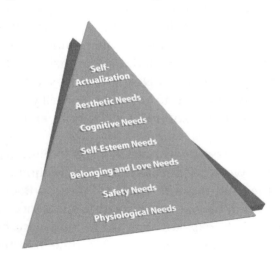

The first four needs – physiological, safety, belonging and self-esteem – are deficiency needs. That is to say they are needs that need to be met so an individual can grow as an individual, represented by the remaining needs.

Physiological needs include things like breathing, hunger, thirst, the right vitamins and nutrients, bodily comforts and so on. Safety needs include the need for structure, feeling secure in your surroundings and having stability in your life. Belonging needs are the needs to be socially accepted and to be loved. Having friends, a sense of community and affectionate relationships are all examples of belonging needs. The last deficiency need is self-esteem needs. There are two levels of self-esteem needs. The lower level is the need for respect from other people, status, recognition, attention, reputation, appreciation and dignity. The higher-level self-esteem need is internal: it is the need for self-respect, self-confidence, achievement, competence, independence and freedom.

If these needs are not met, then future growth is not possible. If you are deficient in one of these needs, then you will seek to fulfil it, and you will not be satisfied until it is met. Once it has been met, though, it will cease to be a source of motivation. When one of these needs is not fulfilled, it can trigger the stress mechanism I referred to earlier in the book, but this time it can be the source of serious neurosis. It might explain why badly behaved children often seem satisfied with their behaviour – it fulfils both belonging and self-esteem needs because they get recognition and a role to play in their community that they may feel they are unable to get by more positive means.

Maslow's growth needs are divided into two levels. The first level contains our cognitive and aesthetic needs. Cognitive needs focus on learning, understanding and exploring. Aesthetic needs are the appreciation of art, order (think especially maths, science and languages) and beauty. Note the left- and right-brain focus of both these needs. They are creative and intellectual, and they are what go on in our classrooms all the time.

The higher level of growth need is self-actualization. This one is a lot less clearly defined than the other levels. It is different because once found, these needs continue to motivate and be felt. It is basically when you realize your potential. It has also been suggested that self-transcendence, when you help other people find self-fulfilment and realize their potential, should be added to the top of the hierarchy.

It is worth pointing out that few people achieve complete self-actualization, but what about the rest? A creative school will be one that seeks to provide the best possible opportunities for pupils, and staff, to explore and improve their abilities – to grow. And to do so it must make sure that, where it can, it caters for all levels of needs. You can hardly expect a pupil to learn (cognitive needs) if he or she is lacking in the first four needs.

How might the creative school accommodate Maslow's Hierarchy of Needs?

Physiological needs: some ideas

♦ breakfast club

♦ healthy food in the canteen

♦ water in the classrooms

♦ parents' cookery classes

♦ room check

The physiological need is not just to provide food and drinks, but to provide the right sustenance. While we know that a healthy, balanced diet is easy to provide, getting pupils to eat it is another matter. Moreover, it seems rather uncertain about whether or not fizzy drinks and chocolate are good or bad for pupils because tests regularly demonstrate different findings! With the government's recent directives about the kind of food that must be served in schools, it looks like schools will now start to meet the healthy food need. Something of a school project could ensue from this. Not only could pupils learn about what's good and bad for them, but you could also combine the activity with an enterprise project to promote imaginary brands of healthy food.

But what about your tuck shop? Now there isn't a lot to stop pupils buying their own supply of sweets and chocolate from the newsagent down the road, so there is little point in the ban on selling chocolates in your school. Not that chocolate is particularly bad for most pupils. While too much chocolate is definitely bad for health and brainpower, research suggests that a little bit of chocolate can give pupils a bit of a boost when it comes to mental energy. However, you should ensure that the sale of fruit, smoothies and cereal bars is easily available because these are definitely good for health and brainpower. Moreover, the sale of fair trade goods will help to meet a social affiliation/belonging need.

While food and drink are primary physiological needs that schools can meet with some reasonably straightforward innovation, there are other needs too. The physical environment within the classroom and around the school can cover many needs (for instance, an aesthetic need), but most basically if it is too hot, too stuffy, too cramped, too dark or too cold, then pupils' focus will rightly be on their discomfort rather than on your lesson. While a teacher can be responsible for a good room layout and keeping it tidy and well-ordered, more fundamental issues are a school management responsibility. Unfortunately, school managers do not spend as much time in classrooms as you do so make sure they are aware of such problems and have a plan as to how they will address them. There is a classroom evaluation form in the previous section of this book; perhaps this could be distributed to all staff to assess needs across the school.

Safety needs: some ideas

♦ anti-bullying campaigns

♦ friendly atmosphere/ethos

♦ non-threatening teaching staff/positive behaviour management

♦ vertical forms

♦ pupil mentoring/buddying scheme

While a school cannot do very much about a pupil's home life, I would say it was a prerequisite of any successful school to provide a safe, stable environment for its pupils. How can you expect pupils to concentrate on learning if they feel threatened by people in the classes? Or if they are more interested in threatening their classmates because there is little to convince them in the structure and ethos of the school that bad behaviour is less enjoyable than good behaviour?

This is a complex issue that goes well beyond the scope of this book. Suffice it to say that if this is a problem in your school, then action on it must come from senior management. There need to be pupil-led campaigns where they learn about creating a happy community. There need to be teacher action groups to review, develop and implement plans to improve ethos and behaviour. But most of all the initiatives need to come from the top, with the head leading assemblies and being pro-active on the issue.

Belonging needs: some ideas

♦ pupils and staff feeling valued and appreciated

♦ anti-bullying

♦ clubs and societies

♦ sports and music

♦ proactive attempt to be inclusive

If a school is to be creative, then it needs to practise what it preaches. And the best way to demonstrate creativity is to provide a range of opportunities for pupils. Most schools have clubs and interest groups, but how many and of what quality? This is an ideal opportunity to bring in multiple intelligences. Can you group all the clubs, groups and annual activities into the eight multiple intelligences? Are there any intelligences that could be better represented? If not, then give your school an imaginary pat on the back. If there are gaps, then here is a chance to make a real difference and enhance the feeling of belonging, and most likely self-esteem, needs of more pupils than you do already.

On the same note, what about your school's staff? Do they feel valued and part of the community, or are they more isolated? How well do they socialize, in and out of the staff room? How cliquey are they? The way in which senior management deals with the school's staff is very important: not being too detached or abrupt, remembering to smile and say hello, joining them at break time, and so on. It tends to be the little things that make people happy, so things like this can make a big difference. If staff are happier, then their approach to problems will be more positive and they will have a more positive impact on pupils' attitudes as well. If teachers are role models for pupils, then it should be borne in mind that senior management are role models for teachers.

Creative Teaching

Self-esteem needs: some ideas

- display area for work
- school has knowledge of pupils' strengths and acts accordingly
- positive criticism
- merit system
- active recognition for good work/behaviour
- removal of unnecessary negative language
- rapid feedback of work
- use of study skills

This is a wide-ranging area of school life. Adults can often trace their insecurities about their competence in certain areas to the way that they were discouraged or encouraged at school. Personally, I was never very good at Craft, Design and Technology at school. While I was good at designing (my work received a lot of praise), my ability to make anything in the workshop was barely adequate. It was never terrible, I never managed to hurt myself or anyone else and the end product was recognizable and functional. In fact I tended to try very hard to get it right. But my CDT teacher never really gave me much encouragement; in fact he usually just frowned at my efforts. So halfway through that GCSE I gave up and transferred to another GCSE.

It was fortunate that my school was supportive and helped me storm through a different GCSE, but even today I look upon things from IKEA with suspicion! I usually give DIY work to someone else to do for fear of messing it up. Don't get me wrong, I don't blame my CDT teacher for my dislike of home maintenance; today I am quite capable of making my own decisions and attempts on these things. But my confidence, and possibly abilities, might be greater when doing so if he had been a little more supportive and encouraging. Teenage minds are very open to your feedback, both positive and negative, and it is important that we build people up rather than bring them down.

A lot of the bullet points above follow on from the contents of this book and need no other explanation. A few do though. The removal of unnecessary negative language refers to things like signs that say 'Do not run in the corridor', which can seem rather authoritarian and therefore something to be derided or a rule to be broken. I suggest it becomes 'For safety reasons, do not run in the corridor, please' or 'For safety reasons, walk in the corridor, please'.

It is worth mentioning merit systems and other ways to recognize achievements. First there must be a system to recognize achievement in your school. For instance, if there are slips of paper to complain about poor work, there must also be slips of paper to commend good work. If there is a merit system, it must be easy to add points for good work. Is there a display board in your department or in prominent places around the school to put up good work? Ask pupils to assess themselves more often – get them to identify two things they think they did well in their work and maybe one thing they think they could do better, then give them feedback focused on how much you agree with the points they identified. And then highlight what else they did well too.

It can be a good idea to have a house system too. Many schools abandoned these because they thought they were divisive, but I disagree. They can aid safety, belonging and esteem needs through fun inter-house competitions (think talent shows and sports day as well as maths challenge days, entrepreneurship and other subject-based competitions), and vertical forms where pupils are grouped by house and not by age – this then enables a good mentoring system between older and younger pupils.

Cognitive needs: some ideas

♦ students know how to learn

♦ use of study skills

- use of formative assessment
- use of VAK and multiple intelligences in teaching
- regular revision built into the timetable/curriculum
- knowledge of students' preferred learning styles
- pupil-centred approach to teaching and learning
- opportunities to get involved with subject material and the learning process

These points should be fairly self-explanatory by now. But these things really work best when they are not employed by teachers in isolation from each other. A school-wide approach that motivates and enables pupils and staff to do these things is the best way to encourage creativity and academic success – i.e. schools that have study skills days, have courses built in across the curriculum to build on these learning skills, to give teachers time to work as a department on developing exciting new lessons, to make sure that pupils build a continuous review of their work into their homework schedules, to make sure that the food on offer is suitable and to make sure that everything that can be done is being done to ensure pupils and staff enjoy being at school. Do this and you will find that pupils will be ready and more able to think creatively and improve their learning performance.

Have you got any questions? Please feel free to email me to discuss anything you've read in this book. My email address is david@learningperformance.com.

Index

Diagrams are given in italics

Creative Teaching